Contents

Emily Jane Brontë

Everyman's Poetry

Everyman, I will go with thee,
and be thy guide

The Brontës

Selected and edited by PAMELA NORRIS

EVERYMAN
J. M. Dent · London

For my mother, Patricia Norris

Text copyright for the poems of Emily Jane Brontë © Pamela Norris 1997
(with the exception of the 1846 texts)
Selection, introduction and other critical apparatus © J. M. Dent 1997

J. M. Dent
Orion Publishing Group
Orion House
5 Upper St Martin's Lane
London WC2H 9EA

7 9 10 8

Typeset by Deltatype Ltd, Birkenhead, Merseyside
Printed in Great Britain by
Clays Ltd, St Ives plc

British Library Cataloguing-in-Publication Data
is available upon request.

ISBN-13 978-0-4608-7864-7

The Orion Publishing Group's policy is to use papers that
are natural, renewable and recyclable products and
made from wood grown in sustainable forests. The logging
and manufacturing processes are expected to conform to
the environmental regulations of the country of origin.

www.orionbooks.co.uk

Anne Brontë

Note on the Authors and Editor

CHARLOTTE, PATRICK BRANWELL, EMILY JANE and ANNE, the four surviving BRONTË children, began at a very early age to write intricate narratives of political struggle, heroism, love and betrayal which revolved around the inhabitants of the imaginary kingdoms that they invented: first the Glasstown sagas, and then Charlotte and Branwell's chronicles of Angria, and Emily and Anne's Gondal stories. All four made attempts to earn their livings outside the small Yorkshire town of Haworth where they grew up, the girls working as teachers and governesses, Branwell as portrait painter, clerk with the Leeds and Manchester Railway, and as a private tutor. After the failure of their joint *Poems* by Currer, Ellis and Acton Bell in 1846, the three sisters began to achieve literary notoriety with the publication of their first novels in 1847, Charlotte's *Jane Eyre*, Emily's *Wuthering Heights* and Anne's less sensational *Agnes Grey*. Anne's second novel, *The Tenant of Wildfell Hall* (1848), stimulated debate through its frank treatment of a woman forced to hide from her alcoholic husband. The failure of Branwell's love affair with a married woman and the decline in his once apparently brilliant prospects led to opium and alcohol addiction, and he died in 1848 of consumption. Within eight months, both Emily and Anne had also died, leaving Charlotte to struggle on with the completion of her second novel, *Shirley* (1849). Her most accomplished work, *Villette*, was published in 1853. Charlotte married Arthur Bell Nicholls, her father's curate, but died a few months later, in 1855.

PAMELA NORRIS is a writer and critic who specialises in women's history and writing. Her publications include *The Story of Eve*, a history of the biblical Eve in myth, literature and art, an anthology of Victorian women poets, and critical editions of Jane Austen and Thomas Hardy for Everyman. *Words of Love: Passionate Women from Heloise to Sylvia Plath* will be published in June 2006.

Chronology of the Brontës' Lives

AB = Anne   CB = Charlotte   EJB = Emily   PB = Patrick   PBB = Branwell

Year	Age	Lives
1816		21 Apl: Birth of CB, third daughter of Rev Patrick and Mrs Maria Brontë, at Thornton, near Bradford, Yorkshire
1817		26 Jun: Birth of PBB, fourth child and only son
1818		30 Jul: Birth of EJB
1820		17 Jan: Birth of AB, sixth and last child
		20 Apl: Brontë family move to Haworth on PB's appointment to the perpetual curacy
1821	38	15 Sept: Death of Mrs Maria Brontë of cancer; her elder sister, Elizabeth Branwell, moves to parsonage to look after Brontë family
1824	10/9	1 Jul: Maria and Elizabeth, two eldest Brontë sisters, sent to board at the Clergy Daughters' School, Cowan Bridge
	8	10 Aug: CB to Clergy Daughters' School
	6	25 Nov: EJB joins her sisters
1825	11	6 May: Death of Maria, at Haworth, of tuberculosis contracted at school
		31 May: Elizabeth sent home with tuberculosis
		1 Jun: PB withdraws CB and EJB from the school
	10	15 Jun: Death of Elizabeth, at Haworth
1826		5 June: PB returns from Leeds with the toy soldiers which inspire the creation of an imaginary world, Glasstown. The children begin to write plays, stories and poems in tiny hand-made books
1831	14	17 Jan: CB goes to Roe Head School, Mirfield, Yorkshire
1832	16	May: CB leaves Roe Head; begins to teach her sisters at home

Chronology of their Times

Year	Literary Context	Historical Events
1816	Walter Scott *Old Mortality*; Lord Byron Canto 1 *Childe Harold*	[Regency in Britain during madness of George III 1809–20]
1817	Death of Jane Austen	
1818	John Keats *Endymion*	Peterloo massacre (1819)
1820	Percy Pysshe Shelley *Prometheus Unbound*	Death of George III; accession George IV; Cato Street conspiracy
1821	Death of John Keats Death of Percy Bysshe Shelley (1822)	Greek war of independence Monroe doctrine enunciated in US (1823)
1824	Death of Lord Byron	
1825		Opening of first passenger steam railway in England, leading to railway building boom
1826		Roman Catholic Relief Act (1829); accession of William IV (1830); revolutions in Europe (1830)
1832	Deaths of Walter Scott and J. W. Goethe	Reform Act (1832) Abolition of slavery in British Empire (1833)

Year	Age	Lives
1834	17/16	Jan: CB and PBB create a new kingdom, Angria. EJB and AB found the imaginary world, Gondal
1835	17–18	PBB training as a professional portrait painter with a view to entering the Royal Academy; plan eventually abandoned
	19/17	29 Jul: CB returns to Roe Head as a teacher, taking EJB with her as a pupil
	15	Mid Oct: EJB, unable to settle at Roe Head, returns to Haworth; her place is taken by AB
1837	17	Dec: AB falls seriously ill at Roe Head; CB resigns her post and withdraws AB from school
1838	20	May: PBB sets up as portrait painter in Bradford
		Sept: EJB takes up a post as teacher in a girls' boarding school at Law Hill, Halifax
1839	21	Feb: PBB abandons his career as an artist
	19	Apl: AB becomes governess to the Ingham family at Blake Hall, Mirfield
	23	May–Jul: CB acts as temporary governess to the Sidgwick family at Stonegappe, Lothersdale
	19	Dec: AB dismissed from her post at Blake Hall
1840	22	Jan: PBB becomes tutor to Postlethwaite family at Broughton-in-Furness, Lake District
	20	May: AB appointed governess to the Robinson family at Thorp Green, near York
	22	Jun: PBB dismissed by the Postlethwaites
	23	Oct: PBB begins work as assistant Clerk-in-Charge on the Leeds-Manchester railway at Sowerby Bridge station near Halifax
1841	24	Mar: CB appointed governess to the White family at Upperwood House, Rawdon, near Leeds
	23	Apl: PBB promoted to Clerk-in-Charge at Luddenden Foot station near Sowerby Bridge
	23	5 Jun: The *Halifax Guardian* publishes the first of twelve poems by PBB
	25	Dec: CB resigns her post at Upperwood House

Year	Literary Context	Historical Events
1834	Deaths of Samuel Taylor Coleridge and Charles Lamb	Factory Act limiting employment of children (1833); Poor Law Amendment Act and trial of 'Tolpuddle Martyrs' (1834)
1837	Charles Dickens *Oliver Twist*	Accession of Queen Victoria; rebellion in Canada
1838		'People's Charter' demands universal male suffrage and parliamentary reform
1839	Harriet Martineau *Deerbrook*	Series of bad harvests and severe depression of trade lead to the 'hungry forties' (1839–43); Chartist National Convention leads to riots and strikes
1840		Britain annexes New Zealand; first postage stamps issued; Union of Upper and Lower Canada
1841	Robert Browning *Bells and Pomegranates*; H. W. Longfellow *Ballads and Other Poems*	Robert Peel Prime Minister (1841–6)

Year	Age	Lives
1842	64/25/23	8 Feb: PB escorts CB and EJB to Brussels where they enter the Pensionnat Heger as pupils
	24	31 Mar: PBB dismissed from railway for failing to keep proper accounts
	66	29 Oct: Death of 'Aunt' Elizabeth Branwell
	26/24	5 Nov: CB and EJB leave Brussels for home on hearing of Aunt Branwell's illness and death
1843	26	27 Jan: CB returns alone to Brussels
1844	27	1 Jan: CB leaves Brussels with a diploma from Monsieur Heger with whom she has fallen in love
	25	July–Oct: sisters' plans for boarding school at the parsonage fail for lack of pupils
1845	26	25 May: Rev Arthur Bell Nicholls comes to Haworth as curate to PB
		11 Jun: AB resigns her post at Thorp Green
	28	Jul: PBB dismissed from Thorp Green when his liaison with Mrs Robinson is discovered
	29	Oct: CB discovers EJB's poems and persuades her sisters to publish a joint collection; they each begin to write a novel
1846		May: Publication of *Poems* by Currer, Ellis and Acton Bell by Aylott & Jones: despite some good reviews only two copies are sold
	30	25 Aug: CB begins second novel, *Jane Eyre*, while nursing her father after a cataract operation
1847	27	Jun: AB completes second novel, *The Tenant of Wildfell Hall*; PBB last poem in *Halifax Guardian*
	28/27	Jul: T. C. Newby accepts EJB's *Wuthering Heights* and AB's *Agnes Grey* for publication but rejects CB's first novel, *The Professor*
	31	Aug: Smith, Elder & Co accept *Jane Eyre*
	31	16 Oct: Publication of *Jane Eyre* to instant success; three editions printed in six months
	29/27	Dec: Publication of *Wuthering Heights* and *Agnes Grey*; Newby suggests they are by Currer Bell

Year	Literary Context	Historical Events
1843	Death of Robert Southey	
1844		Second railway boom (1844–7)
1845		Irish famine; US annexes Texas; J. H. Newman, founder of Oxford movement, becomes a Roman Catholic
1846		Britain repeals corn laws; Mexican war begins
1847	W. M. Thackeray *Vanity Fair* (1847–8)	Factory Act limits children and women to ten-hour working day

Year	Age	Lives
1848	28/32	Jul: Publication, by Newby, of AB's *The Tenant of Wildfell Hall*. CB and AB go to London to prove their separate identities
	31	24 Sept: Death of PBB from tuberculosis
		Nov: Re-issue of *Poems* by Currer, Ellis & Acton Bell by Smith, Elder & Co
	30	19 Dec: Death of EJB from tuberculosis
1849	29	28 May: Death of AB from tuberculosis at Scarborough
	33	28 Aug: CB completes her third novel, *Shirley*
		26 Oct: Publication of *Shirley*
		Dec: CB stays with George Smith in London; meets W. M. Thackeray and Harriet Martineau
1850	34	May–Jul: CB in London; sits for her portrait to George Richmond, then travels to Edinburgh with the Smiths
		Aug: CB meets Mrs Gaskell
		10 Dec: Smith, Elder & Co publish a single volume edition of *Wuthering Heights* and *Agnes Grey* with a biographical preface by CB
1851		Apl: James Taylor of Smith, Elder & Co, proposes to CB, but is refused and goes to India
	35	May–Jun: CB stays with Smiths in London, going to Thackeray's lectures, the theatre and the Great Exhibition; visits Mrs Gaskell in Manchester
		Nov: CB begins her fourth novel, *Villette*
1852	36	Nov: CB completes *Villette*
	33	13 Dec: Rev Arthur Bell Nicholls proposes to Charlotte, but is refused at PB's insistence
1853	36	Jan–Feb: CB stays with Smiths in London for a month for publication of *Villette*
	37	Apl: CB visits Mrs Gaskell in Manchester
	34	May: Arthur Bell Nicholls leaves Haworth
		Sept: Mrs Gaskell stays with Charlotte

Year	Literary Context	Historical Events
1848	Mrs Gaskell *Mary Barton*; Marx and Engels *Communist Manifesto*	'Year of Revolution' in Europe; proclamation of Third Republic in France
1849	Charles Dickens *David Copperfield*; death of Hartley Coleridge	
1850	Death of William Wordsworth; Elizabeth Barrett Browning *Sonnets from the Portuguese*	Death of Robert Peel
1851	John Ruskin *The Stones of Venice* (1851–3)	Great Exhibition in London
1852	Harriet Beecher Stowe *Uncle Tom's Cabin*	Fall of French Republic, Napoleon III becomes emperor
1853	Mrs Gaskell *Ruth*	Livingstone begins African explorations; Factory Act extends ten-hour working day to men

Year	Age	Lives
1854	37/35	Apl: CB officially engaged to Arthur Bell Nicholls
		May: CB visits Mrs Gaskell in Manchester
	38/35	29 Jun: CB marries Arthur Bell Nicholls in Haworth church: they honeymoon in Ireland then live with PB at Haworth Parsonage
1855	39	31 Mar: CB dies in the early stages of pregnancy
		Jul: PB asks Mrs Gaskell to write CB's biography
1857		25 Mar: Publication of Mrs Gaskell's *Life of CB*
		6 Jun: First publication of *The Professor*
1860		Apl: CB's fragment, *Emma*, published in *The Cornhill Magazine* with preface by Thackeray
1861	84/42	7 Jun: Death of PB; Arthur Bell Nicholls retires from church and returns to Ireland

Year	Literary Context	Historical Events
1854	Charles Dickens *Hard Times*	Crimean War begins; Florence Nightingale goes to nurse in the Crimea; Oxford and Cambridge opened up to dissenters from Church of England
1855		Treaty of Paris ends Crimean War (1856)
1857	Anthony Trollope *Barchester Towers*	Indian mutiny
1860	George Eliot *The Mill on the Floss*	
1861	Death of Elizabeth Barrett Browning	Death of Prince Albert; American Civil War begins

Introduction

The popular myth of the Brontë family – the four brilliant children feverishly scribbling in the chilly parsonage, doomed alike by the infectious vapours seeping from the graves that crowded against their living-room windows and the piercing winds of the gaunt moors that pressed against the rear of the house – is too seductive ever to be entirely quashed. But even a brief glance at their poetry and the circumstances in which it was written disturbs this cosy fantasy. The notion that the four surviving Brontë siblings were essentially the same identity variously bodied is confounded by the differences in the subject matter and style of their work; their confined existence in solitary Haworth is similarly disproved by the variety of places and situations in which the poems were written. Many of the poems deal with reality, lived out individually and in a number of locations, the harsh facts of life that Charlotte was ruefully to describe in the first pages of her novel *Shirley* as, 'Something real, cool, and solid ... unromantic as Monday morning'. The Brontës wrote from personal experience about loneliness and intellectual isolation, the necessity to endure uncongenial work, about unrequited desire and the death of loved ones, the pain of exile and the intense longing for home. There are lighter moments, in particular the zest of windy or stormy days, the beauty of the natural world, and the power of memory to recreate past happiness.

A sharp distinction between fantasy and reality is, however, inappropriate where the Brontës are concerned: in one of her more famous poems, 'Retrospection', Charlotte recalls, 'We wove a web in childhood, / A web of sunny air', and many of the poems seem to spring as much from an intense imaginative identification with the fictitious worlds that they devised in early childhood as from the everyday events that are their apparent inspiration: from Charlotte and Branwell's warfaring kingdom of Angria, and Emily and Anne's Gondal with its passionate, wilful queen, the beautiful Augusta Almeda. Branwell writes a number of poems in the persona of his favourite hero, Alexander Percy, and who can say, in these poems, whether it is Branwell speaking, using the convenient disguise of a fictitious character, or his alter ego Percy, brought alive by Branwell's talent for mimicry and improvisation? Could Branwell himself have made the distinction? The question of what is 'real' and what 'made up' is often puzzling where the Brontës are concerned, and their customary blurring of the boundary between the two was to have a direct effect on both Charlotte and Branwell's lives. For both of them, their interior worlds seemed at times to manufacture the circumstances of their lives, rather than their work deriving from experience as is so often conjectured. It could be argued that Charlotte's early preoccupation in her fiction with bullying men and masochistic females was the source of her real-life obsession with her Brussels teacher and colleague, Constantin Heger. Branwell's encounter with Mrs Robinson, the wife of his employer when he was a tutor at Thorp Green, and his collapse into alcoholism after their affair was discovered, can be similarly construed as a projection of childhood fantasies. All four Brontës had long inhabited invented worlds in which men openly expressed violent emotions, and typically took to drink and debauchery to recover from adverse fortune; Branwell was simply following his own imaginary role-models. In the poems in this collection, it is often impossible to know how far the writer is speaking personally or assuming a role, and in a sense it doesn't matter. What is important is the use that the writers made of the close interaction between their inner and outer worlds. Except for the more resolutely grounded Anne, the Brontës' web of fantasy seems to have overlain every aspect of their lives, and Emily's Augusta Almeda remembering her dead lover is just as emotionally persuasive as the governess Anne Brontë pining for her family life at Haworth Parsonage.

As poets, there are clear differences between the four Brontës. In his introduction to Branwell's translation of the Odes of Horace, John Drinkwater wrote of Emily and Branwell: 'These two had the wildness, the sense of loneliness, the ache for some indefinable thing called freedom, that mark the poet from infancy', but Emily is consistently a better poet than Branwell, whose writing is too often vitiated by the failure of conviction that was characteristic of his behaviour in everyday life. Although impressively versatile in form and genre, many of his poems lack polish, the final push of thought that would lift style and language out of the ordinary or half-baked into art. 'Poor, brilliant, gay, moody, moping, wildly excitable, miserable Brontë!' as his friend Francis Grundy described him: perhaps if he had found the poetic mentor that he sought, or even a network of talented young writers outside his own family with whom to discuss his work and ideas, Branwell might have become a substantial poet. Even so, there are sufficient pleasures – and surprises – to make his poetry well worth reading. Among his most accomplished works are the fine translations of the Odes of Horace, which demonstrate a felicitous harmony of language, metre and subject matter, and indicate what, at his best, Branwell was capable of producing, represented here by 'To Sestius'. Death – so persistent a feature of Branwell and Charlotte's Angrian chronicles, with their bloody civil wars, assassinations and suicides – is the theme of 'On Caroline', in which an unidentified narrator mourns for a young girl, possibly Branwell's own sister Maria who died of consumption when Branwell was seven. Here Branwell uses the standard features of gothic romance to establish atmosphere: the poem is set in an ancestral hall which Caroline will no longer illuminate by her smile, any more than the sun can penetrate the 'raven-pinioned dream / Of coffin, shroud, and sepulchre' of the sleep-entranced watcher by her deathbed, so reminiscent of the Baron and his warrior-guests in Keats's 'Eve of St Agnes', who are gripped by foreboding nightmares 'Of witch, and demon, and large coffin-worm' as the heroine Madeline flees at dead of night with her seducer Porphyro. But Branwell's main preoccupation in this poem is to point out the selective power of memory, which tenaciously retains the image of unhappiness long after pleasure has been forgotten. One of Branwell's most interesting death poems is the 'Epistle From a Father to a Child in Her Grave', which the Brontë biographer Juliet Barker hypothesises may have been inspired by the death of a natural daughter of Branwell's (see Notes). Characteristically, this poem dwells on the unhappiness of the living which the dead are spared, and suggests the influence of Wordsworth in its comparisons between implacable, persistent nature and individual human feeling and destiny. Also Wordsworthian is 'Penmænmawr', written some months after Branwell's abrupt dismissal from Thorp Green when his affair with Lydia Robinson had been discovered, which expresses the longing to stand firm in the face of stormy weather.

Branwell's companion in fantasy, his older sister Charlotte, is at her best only competent as a poet, and her bent towards elaborate storytelling can overburden the narrative verse form. Not for her the speaking phrase or lightning character sketch, and her appetite for stock characters, for long-suffering heroines and domineering or villainous men, so powerfully metamorphosed into the great romances of *Jane Eyre* and *Villette*, strain credibility in her earlier works. Part of the problem is the difficulty of handling a complex narrative in a comparatively short poem, which Charlotte never fully masters, and her greatest poetic effects are achieved in the more leisured prose of the novels. Her use of 'poetic' language also strains her verse, so that meaning is crushed beneath overwrought manner, and her poetry is most persuasive when she forgets self-conscious artistry in the interest of communicating an intellectual idea or personal emotion. The short extract from 'Retrospection' shows Charlotte in full control of her material: it builds visually on a series of simple, fruitful images – the web, the spring, the mustard seed and almond rod – to convey the rich profusion of stories that sprang from the Brontës' childhood fantasies, and ends by reminding the reader of how powerfully those narratives still influence the adult Charlotte. 'The Teacher's Monologue' allows the reader to step into Charlotte's confined existence as a teacher at the Roe Head school, and to share her bitter reflections on the 'yoke' of enforced employment, the yearning for home, and the painful sense that time is flying past with nothing achieved. 'The Autumn day its course has run', a fragment scribbled in Charlotte's Brussels exercise book, atmospherically recreates the intense pleasure of solitary musing. In 'He saw my heart's woe', the angry female persona of the novels emerges, the passionate young woman who lacerates her soul by dashing it against the 'Granite God', variously represented in Charlotte's fiction and life by the inscrutable Paul Emanuel, alias Edward Rochester, alias Charlotte's Brussels tutor and colleague M. Constantin Heger. The two final poems in this selection were written soon after the death of each of Charlotte's younger sisters. The poem on Emily claims grief but is unconvincing, and perhaps reflects Charlotte's troubled relationship with her sister, as well as bafflement at Emily's behaviour in the months leading up to her death, her stoic refusal to accept treatment for her illness or any special attentions from her family. Anne's patient death in Scarborough, after submitting to every care the doctors and her family could offer, was perhaps easier both to bear and to grieve over.

Of the four Brontës, Anne appears to have written most openly from the heart. The role-playing so assiduously explored by Branwell, and so essential a part of Emily's poetic output that it is impossible to say what is 'real' and what assumed, seems to have been largely abandoned by Anne, whose surviving poems are typically brief, fluent expressions of emotion. She writes feelingly of homesickness and exile ('The Consolation', 'Home') and imprisonment ('The Captive Dove'); of the struggle for faith ('Despondency', 'A Prayer'), and occasional, overwhelming joy in God ('In Memory of a Happy Day in February'); of delight in nature and her pleasure in flowers ('Lines Composed in a Wood on a Windy Day', 'Lines Written at Thorp Green'); of the absence or death of the (unnamed) beloved ('Appeal', 'A Reminiscence'); and, unexpectedly, of maternal longings ('Dreams'). Particularly moving are her 'Last Lines', written soon after Anne learned that she too was suffering from the disease that had just killed Emily. Her poems suggest a sensitive and watchful personality, strengthened by a powerful sense of decorum and a self-disciplined withholding of her troubles from her family and the strangers who employed her as governess to their children. The conscientious struggle to do her duty as a Christian combined with the passionate longing to be claimed by God make her a natural precursor to Christina Rossetti, although she lacks Rossetti's supreme lyric gift and versatility. Surprisingly, given her reticence, what Anne's poetry offers is intimacy, an opportunity to share quiet but intensely felt emotional experience, and it makes possible a more informed reading of her novels, *Agnes Grey* and *The Tenant of Wildfell Hall*. Once she had slipped free from the influence of Emily and the Gondal narratives, unity rather than diversity, and a singleminded approach to life and art, are what characterise Anne's mature writings.

Emily Jane Brontë was a better poet than any of her three siblings, and the best introduction to her work is simply to read the poems. Knowledge of her life and the circumstances in which she wrote is only partly illuminating: of all the Brontës, Emily is the most difficult to pin down. While it is possible to make all kinds of statements about Charlotte and Branwell from the evidence of their voluminous writings, from letters, and the witness of people who knew them, and even about Anne on the basis of her working life as well as her novels and poetry, Emily remains elusive. This is partly because so little of Emily survives outside her poetry. Unlike Charlotte, she did not leave behind an extensive correspondence with friends and publishers; all that remain are a handful of letters and the diary papers that she and Anne wrote periodically as life records to be read four years hence. Emily's papers are surprisingly naive and childish productions, far removed from the linguistic and emotional sophistication of poems such as 'Remembrance' or even the deceptively simple 'Tell me, tell me, smiling child'. It is as if the Emily who wrote poetry and the Emily who lived quietly in the parsonage at Haworth, dividing her time between routine domestic tasks, reading and wandering on the moors, were separate consciousnesses. One clue in the diary papers to the integration of Emily's two worlds are the casual references to the fictitious kingdom of Gondal, which she drops in as if it were as much part of everyday reality as having to peel the potatoes for Aunt Branwell. 'The Gondalians [are] at present in a threatening state', she writes on 30 July 1841, sandwiched between a daydream about the school that the three sisters were hoping to set up, and good resolutions about more systematic reading. For Emily, reality and fantasy appear to have blended, but she chose to communicate her unified vision of the world through poetry, and through her one surviving novel, *Wuthering Heights*. What her poems describe are powerful emotions, of passionate love, of hate and grief and defiance, explored through an often mystical sense of the natural world, and expressed in extraordinarily fluid verse. Emily Brontë's formal control of the tools of her craft, of metre and rhyme, and selection of language, is impressive; her poetic vision and lyricism make her an outstanding poet.

PAMELA NORRIS

The Brontës

Charlotte Brontë

from **Retrospection**

We wove a web in childhood,
    A web of sunny air;
We dug a spring in infancy
    Of water pure and fair;

We sowed in youth a mustard seed,   5
    We cut an almond rod;
We are now grown up to riper age –
    Are they withered in the sod?

Are they blighted, failed and faded,
    Are they mouldered back to clay?   10
For life is darkly shaded;
    And its joys fleet fast away.

Faded! the web is still of air,
    But how its folds are spread,
And from its tints of crimson clear   15
    How deep a glow is shed.
The light of an Italian sky
Where clouds of sunset lingering lie
    Is not more ruby-red.

But the spring was under a mossy stone,   20
    Its jet may gush no more.
Hark! sceptic bid thy doubts be gone,
    Is that a feeble roar
Rushing around thee? Lo! the tide
Of waves where armed fleets may ride   25
Sinking and swelling, frowns and smiles
An ocean with a thousand isles
    And scarce a glimpse of shore.

The mustard-seed in distant land
  Bends down a mighty tree,   30
The dry unbudding almond-wand
  Has touched eternity.
There came a second miracle
Such as on Aaron's sceptre fell,
And sapless grew like life from heath,   35
Bud, bloom and fruit in mingling wreath
All twined the shrivelled off-shoot round
As flowers lie on the lone grave-mound.

Dream that stole o'er us in the time
When life was in its vernal clime,   40
Dream that still faster o'er us steals
  As the mild star of spring declining
The advent of that day reveals,
  That glows in Sirius' fiery shining:
Oh! as thou swellest, and as the scenes   45
  Cover this cold world's darkest features,
Stronger each change my spirit weans
  To bow before thy god-like creatures.

When I sat 'neath a strange roof-tree
With nought I knew or loved round me,   50
Oh how my heart shrank back to thee,
Then I felt how fast thy ties had bound me.

The Teacher's Monologue

The room is quiet, thoughts alone
People its mute tranquillity;
The yoke put off, the long task done, —
I am, as it is bliss to be,
Still and untroubled. Now, I see,   5
For the first time, how soft the day
O'er waveless water, stirless tree,

Silent and sunny, wings its way.
Now, as I watch that distant hill,
So faint, so blue, so far removed,   10
Sweet dreams of home my heart may fill,
That home where I am known and loved:
It lies beyond; yon azure brow
Parts me from all Earth holds for me;
And, morn and eve, my yearnings flow   15
Thitherward tending, changelessly.
My happiest hours, aye! all the time,
I love to keep in memory,
Lapsed among moors, ere life's first prime
Decayed to dark anxiety.   20

Sometimes, I think a narrow heart
Makes me thus mourn those far away,
And keeps my love so far apart
From friends and friendships of today;
Sometimes, I think 'tis but a dream   25
I treasure up so jealously,
All the sweet thoughts I live on seem
To vanish into vacancy:
And then, this strange, coarse world around
Seems all that's palpable and true;   30
And every sight, and every sound,
Combines my spirit to subdue
To aching grief, so void and lone
Is Life and Earth – so worse than vain,
The hopes that, in my own heart sown,   35
And cherished by such sun and rain
As Joy and transient Sorrow shed,
Have ripened to a harvest there:
Alas! methinks I hear it said,
'Thy golden sheaves are empty air.'   40

All fades away; my very home
I think will soon be desolate;
I hear, at times, a warning come
Of bitter partings at its gate;
And, if I should return and see   45

The hearth-fire quenched, the vacant chair;
And hear it whispered mournfully,
That farewells have been spoken there.
What shall I do, and whither turn?
Where look for peace? When cease to mourn?   50

'Tis not the air I wished to play,
    The strain I wished to sing;
My wilful spirit slipped away
    And struck another string.
I neither wanted smile nor tear,   55
    Bright joy nor bitter woe,
But just a song that sweet and clear,
    Though haply sad, might flow.

A quiet song, to solace me
    When sleep refused to come;   60
A strain to chase despondency,
    When sorrowful for home.
In vain I try; I cannot sing;
    All feels so cold and dead;
No wild distress, no gushing spring   65
    Of tears in anguish shed;

But all the impatient gloom of one
    Who waits a distant day,
When, some great task of suffering done,
    Repose shall toil repay.   70
For youth departs, and pleasure flies,
    And life consumes away,
And youth's rejoicing ardour dies
    Beneath this drear delay;

And Patience, weary with her yoke,   75
    Is yielding to despair,
And Health's elastic spring is broke
    Beneath the strain of care.
Life will be gone ere I have lived;
    Where now is Life's first prime?   80

I've worked and studied, longed and grieved,
   Through all that rosy time.

To toil, to think, to long, to grieve, –
   Is such my future fate?
The morn was dreary, must the eve   85
   Be also desolate?
Well, such a life at least makes Death
   A welcome, wished-for friend;
Then, aid me, Reason, Patience, Faith,
   To suffer to the end!   90

Mementos

Arranging long-locked drawers and shelves
Of cabinets, shut up for years,
What a strange task we've set ourselves!
How still the lonely room appears!
How strange this mass of ancient treasures,   5
Mementos of past pains and pleasures;
These volumes, clasped with costly stone,
With print all faded, gilding gone;
These fans of leaves, from Indian trees –
These crimson shells, from Indian seas –   10
These tiny portraits, set in rings –
Once, doubtless, deemed such precious things;
Keepsakes bestowed by Love on Faith,
And worn till the receiver's death,
Now stored with cameos, china, shells,   15
In this old closet's dusty cells.

I scarcely think, for ten long years,
A hand has touched these relics old;
And, coating each, slow-formed, appears,
The growth of green and antique mould.   20

All in this house is mossing over;
All is unused, and dim, and damp;
Nor light, nor warmth, the rooms discover –
Bereft for years of fire and lamp.

The sun, sometimes in summer, enters   25
The casements, with reviving ray;
But the long rains of many winters
Moulder the very walls away.

And outside all is ivy, clinging
To chimney, lattice, gable grey;   30
Scarcely one little red rose springing
Through the green moss can force its way.

Unscared, the daw, and starling nestle,
Where the tall turret rises high,
And winds alone come near to rustle   35
The thick leaves where their cradles lie.

I sometimes think, when late at even
I climb the stair reluctantly,
Some shape that should be well in heaven,
Or ill elsewhere, will pass by me.   40

I fear to see the very faces,
Familiar thirty years ago,
Even in the old accustomed places
Which look so cold and gloomy now.

I've come, to close the window, hither,   45
At twilight, when the sun was down,
And Fear, my very soul would wither,
Lest something should be dimly shown,

Too much the buried form resembling,
Of her who once was mistress here;   50
Lest doubtful shade, or moonbeam trembling,
Might take her aspect, once so dear.

Hers was this chamber; in her time
It seemed to me a pleasant room,
For then no cloud of grief or crime   55
Had cursed it with a settled gloom;

I had not seen death's image laid
In shroud and sheet, on yonder bed.
Before she married, she was blest –
Blest in her youth, blest in her worth;   60
Her mind was calm, its sunny rest
Shone in her eyes more clear than mirth.

And when attired in rich array,
Light, lustrous hair about her brow,
She yonder sat – a kind of day   65
Lit up – what seems so gloomy now.
These grim oak walls, even then were grim;
That old carved chair, was then antique;
But what around looked dusk and dim
Served as a foil to her fresh cheek;   70
Her neck, and arms, of hue so fair,
Eyes of unclouded, smiling, light;
Her soft, and curled, and floating hair,
Gems and attire, as rainbow bright.

Reclined in yonder deep recess,   75
Ofttimes she would, at evening, lie
Watching the sun; she seemed to bless
With happy glance the glorious sky.
She loved such scenes, and as she gazed,
Her face evinced her spirit's mood;   80
Beauty or grandeur ever raised
In her, a deep-felt gratitude.

But of all lovely things, she loved
A cloudless moon, on summer night;
Full oft have I impatience proved   85
To see how long, her still delight
Would find a theme in reverie,
Out on the lawn, or where the trees

Let in the lustre fitfully,
As their boughs parted momently,   90
To the soft, languid, summer breeze.
Alas! that she should e'er have flung
Those pure, though lonely joys away –
Deceived by false and guileful tongue,
She gave her hand, then suffered wrong;   95
Oppressed, ill-used, she faded young,
And died of grief by slow decay.

Open that casket – look how bright
Those jewels flash upon the sight;
The brilliants have not lost a ray   100
Of lustre, since her wedding day.
But see – upon that pearly chain –
How dim lies time's discolouring stain!
I've seen that by her daughter worn:
For, e'er she died, a child was born;   105
A child that ne'er its mother knew,
That lone, and almost friendless grew;
For, ever, when its step drew nigh,
Averted was the father's eye;
And then, a life impure and wild   110
Made him a stranger to his child;
Absorbed in vice, he little cared
On what she did, or how she fared.

The love withheld, she never sought,
She grew uncherished – learnt untaught;   115
To her the inward life of thought
    Full soon was open laid.
I know not if her friendlessness
Did sometimes on her spirit press.
    But plaint she never made.   120
The book-shelves were her darling treasure,
She rarely seemed the time to measure
    While she could read alone.
And she too loved the twilight wood,
And often, in her mother's mood,   125
Away to yonder hill would hie,

Like her, to watch the setting sun,
Or see the stars born, one by one,
   Out of the darkening sky.
Nor would she leave that hill till night 130
Trembled from pole to pole with light;
Even then, upon her homeward way,
Long – long her wandering steps delayed
To quit the sombre forest shade,
Through which her eerie pathway lay. 135
You ask if she had beauty's grace?
I know not – but a nobler face
   My eyes have seldom seen;
A keen and fine intelligence,
And, better still, the truest sense 140
   Were in her speaking mien.
But bloom or lustre was there none,
Only at moments, fitful shone
   An ardour in her eye,
That kindled on her cheek a flush, 145
Warm as a red sky's passing blush
   And quick with energy.
Her speech, too, was not common speech,
No wish to shine, or aim to teach,
   Was in her words displayed: 150
She still began with quiet sense,
But oft the force of eloquence
   Came to her lips in aid;
Language and voice unconscious changed,
And thoughts, in other words arranged, 155
   Her fervid soul transfused
Into the hearts of those who heard,
And transient strength and ardour stirred,
   In minds to strength unused.
Yet in gay crowd or festal glare, 160
Grave and retiring was her air;
'Twas seldom, save with me alone,
That fire of feeling freely shone;
She loved not awe's nor wonder's gaze,
Nor even exaggerated praise, 165
Nor even notice, if too keen

The curious gazer searched her mien.
Nature's own green expanse revealed
The world, the pleasures, she could prize;
On free hill-side, in sunny field,   170
In quiet spots by woods concealed,
Grew wild and fresh her chosen joys,
Yet Nature's feelings deeply lay
In that endowed and youthful frame;
Shrined in her heart and hid from day,   175
They burned unseen with silent flame;
In youth's first search for mental light,
She lived but to reflect and learn,
But soon her mind's maturer might
For stronger task did pant and yearn;   180
And stronger task did fate assign,
Task that a giant's strength might strain;
To suffer long and ne'er repine,
Be calm in frenzy, smile at pain.

Pale with the secret war of feeling,   185
Sustained with courage, mute, yet high;
The wounds at which she bled, revealing
Only by altered cheek and eye;

She bore in silence – but when passion
Surged in her soul with ceaseless foam,   190
The storm at last brought desolation,
And drove her exiled from her home.

And silent still, she straight assembled
The wrecks of strength her soul retained;
For though the wasted body trembled.   195
The unconquered mind, to quail, disdained.

She crossed the sea – now lone she wanders
By Seine's, or Rhine's, or Arno's flow;
Fain would I know if distance renders
Relief or comfort to her woe.   200

Fain would I know if, henceforth, ever,
These eyes shall read in hers again,
That light of love which faded never,
Though dimmed so long with secret pain.

She will return, but cold and altered,   205
Like all whose hopes too soon depart;
Like all on whom have beat, unsheltered,
The bitter blasts that blight the heart.

No more shall I behold her lying
Calm on a pillow, smoothed by me;   210
No more that spirit, worn with sighing,
Will know the rest of infancy.

If still the paths of lore she follow,
'Twill be with tired and goaded will;
She'll only toil, the aching hollow,   215
The joyless blank of life to fill.

And oh! full oft, quite spent and weary,
Her hand will pause, her head decline;
That labour seems so hard and dreary,
On which no ray of hope may shine.   220

Thus the pale blight of time and sorrow
Will shade with grey her soft, dark hair;
Then comes the day that knows no morrow,
And death succeeds to long despair.

So speaks experience, sage and hoary;   225
I see it plainly, know it well,
Like one who, having read a story,
Each incident therein can tell.

Touch not that ring, 'twas his, the sire
    Of that forsaken child;   230
And nought his relics can inspire
    Save memories, sin-defiled.

I, who sat by his wife's death-bed,
   I, who his daughter loved,
Could almost curse the guilty dead,   235
   For woes, the guiltless proved.

And heaven did curse – they found him laid,
   When crime for wrath was ri[p]e,
Cold – with the suicidal blade
   Clutched in his desperate gripe.   240

'Twas near that long deserted hut,
   Which in the wood decays,
Death's axe, self-wielded, struck his root,
   And lopped his desperate days.

You know the spot, where three black trees,   245
   Lift up their branches fell,
And moaning, ceaseless as the seas,
Still seem, in every passing breeze,
   The deed of blood to tell.

They named him mad, and laid his bones   250
   Where holier ashes lie;
Yet doubt not that his spirit groans,
   In hell's eternity.

But, lo! night, closing o'er the earth,
   Infects our thoughts with gloom;   255
Come, let us strive to rally mirth,
Where glows a clear and tranquil hearth
   In some more cheerful room.

Parting

There's no use in weeping,
Though we are condemned to part:
There's such a thing as keeping
A remembrance in one's heart:

There's such a thing as dwelling   5
On the thought ourselves have nurs'd,
And with scorn and courage telling
The world to do its worst.

We'll not let its follies grieve us,
We'll just take them as they come;   10
And then every day will leave us
A merry laugh for home.

When we've left each friend and brother,
When we're parted wide and far,
We will think of one another,   15
As even better than we are.

Every glorious sight above us,
Every pleasant sight beneath,
We'll connect with those that love us,
Whom we truly love till death!   20

In the evening, when we're sitting
By the fire perchance alone,
Then shall heart with warm heart meeting,
Give responsive tone for tone.

We can burst the bonds which chain us,   25
Which cold human hands have wrought,
And where none shall dare restrain us
We can meet again, in thought.

So there's no use in weeping,
Bear a cheerful spirit still;   30
Never doubt that Fate is keeping
Future good for present ill!

Life

Life, believe, is not a dream
  So dark as sages say;
Oft a little morning rain
  Foretells a pleasant day.
Sometimes there are clouds of gloom,   5
  But these are transient all;
If the shower will make the roses bloom,
  O why lament its fall?
    Rapidly, merrily,
  Life's sunny hours flit by,   10
    Gratefully, cheerily,
  Enjoy them as they fly!

What though Death at times steps in,
  And calls our Best away?
What though sorrow seems to win,   15
  O'er hope, a heavy sway?
Yet hope again elastic springs,
  Unconquered, though she fell;
Still buoyant are her golden wings,
  Still strong to bear us well.   20
    Manfully, fearlessly,
  The day of trial bear,
    For gloriously, victoriously,
  Can courage quell despair!

'The Autumn day its course has run'

The Autumn day its course has run – the Autumn evening falls;
Already risen, the Autumn moon gleams quiet on these walls
And Twilight to my lonely house a silent guest is come –
In mask of gloom through every room she passes dusk and dumb.
Her veil is spread, her shadow shed o'er stair and chamber void, 5
And now I feel her presence steal even to my lone fireside.
Sit, silent Nun – sit there and be
Comrade and Confidant to me.

'Early wrapt in slumber deep'

Early wrapt in slumber deep
 Rest the serving-men;
Master, dame, and hand-maid sleep
 Sound, at Bonny glen.

Time's dark stream, in yonder vales,   5
 Glides with shadowed flow;
O'er each latticed window falls
 A drapery, sweeping low.

While, within the house, is spread
 Shade o'er weary eyes,   10
Screenless, in his out-door shed,
 A little herd-boy lies.

Splendid light from summer moon
 Falls on each green tree;
Soft as twilight, clear as noon,   15
 Smiles each dewy lea.

Water in the clear brook flows
    Fast, with trembling brightness;
By its side, the causeways shews
    A track of silver whiteness.   20

'He saw my heart's woe'

He saw my heart's woe, discovered my soul's anguish,
    How in fever, in thirst, in atrophy it pined;
Knew he could heal, yet looked and let it languish, –
    To its moans spirit-deaf, to its pangs spirit-blind.

But once a year he heard a whisper low and dreary   5
    Appealing for aid, entreating some reply;
Only when sick, soul-worn, and torture-weary,
    Breathed I that prayer, heaved I that sigh.

He was mute as is the grave, he stood stirless as a tower;
    At last I looked up, and saw I prayed to stone: 10
I asked help of that which to help had no power,
    I sought love where love was utterly unknown.

Idolater I kneeled to an idol cut in rock!
    I might have slashed my flesh and drawn my heart's best
        blood:
The Granite God had felt no tenderness, no shock;   15
    My Baal had not seen nor heard nor understood.

In dark remorse I rose; I rose in darker shame;
    Self-condemned I withdrew to an exile from my kind;
A solitude I sought where mortal never came,
    Hoping in its wilds forgetfulness to find.   20

Now, Heaven, heal the wound which I still deeply feel;
    Thy glorious hosts look not in scorn on our poor race;
Thy King eternal doth no iron judgment deal
    On suffering worms who seek forgiveness, comfort, grace.

He gave our hearts to love: He will not love despise,   25
    E'en if the gift be lost, as mine was long ago;
He will forgive the fault, will bid the offender rise,
    Wash out with dews of bliss the fiery brand of woe;

And give a sheltered place beneath the unsullied throne,
    Whence the soul redeemed may mark Time's fleeting course
      round earth;   30
And knows its trials overpast, its sufferings gone,
    And feel the peril past of Death's immortal birth.

On the Death of
Emily Jane Brontë

My darling, thou wilt never know
The grinding agony of woe
    That we have borne for thee.
Thus may we consolation tear
E'en from the depth of our despair   5
    And wasting misery.

The nightly anguish thou art spared
When all the crushing truth is bared
    To the awakening mind,
When the galled heart is pierced with grief,   10
Till wildly it implores relief,
    But small relief can find.

Nor know'st thou what it is to lie
Looking forth with streaming eye
    On life's lone wilderness.   15
'Weary, weary, dark and drear,
How shall I the journey bear,
    The burden and distress?'

Then since thou art spared such pain
We will not wish thee here again;   20
  He that lives must mourn.
God help us through our misery
And give us rest and joy with thee
  When we reach our bourne!

On the Death of Anne Brontë

There's little joy in life for me,
  And little terror in the grave;
I've lived the parting hour to see
  Of one I would have died to save.

Calmly to watch the failing breath,   5
  Wishing each sigh might be the last;
Longing to see the shade of death
  O'er those beloved features cast.

The cloud, the stillness that must part
  The darling of my life from me;   10
And then to thank God from my heart,
  To thank Him well and fervently;

Although I knew that we had lost
  The hope and glory of our life;
And now, benighted, tempest-tossed,   15
  Must bear alone the weary strife.

Patrick Branwell Brontë

Augusta

Augusta! Though I'm far away
   Across the dark blue sea,
Still eve and morn and night and day
   Will I remember Thee!

And, though I cannot see thee nigh   5
   Or hear thee speak to me,
Thy look and voice and memory
   Shall not forgotten be.

I stand upon this Island shore,
   A single hour alone,   10
And see the Atlantic swell before
   With sullen surging tone,

While high in heaven the full Moon glides
   Above the breezy deep,
Unmoved by waves or winds or tides   15
   That far beneath her sweep.

She marches through this midnight air,
   So silent and divine,
With not a wreath of vapour there
   To dim her silver shine.   20

For every cloud through ether driven
   Has settled far below,
And round the unmeasured skirts of heaven
   Their whitened fleeces glow.

They join and part and pass away   25
   Beyond the heaving sea,

So mutable and restless they,
  So still and changeless she.

Those clouds have melted into air,
  Those waves have sunk to sleep,   30
But clouds renewed are rising there,
  And fresh waves crowd the deep.

How like the chaos of my soul,
  Where visions ever rise,
And thoughts and passions ceaseless roll,   35
  And tumult never dies.

Each fancy but the former's grave
  And germ of that to come,
While all are fleeting as the wave
  That chafes itself to foam.   40

I said that full Moon glides on high,
  Howe'er the world repines,
And in its own untroubled sky
  For ever smiles and shines.

So dark'ning o'er my anxious brow,   45
  Though thicken cares and pain,
Within my Heart Augusta thou
  For ever shalt remain.

And Thou art not that wintry moon
  With its melancholy ray,   50
But where thou shinest is summer noon
  And bright and perfect day.

The Moon sinks down as sinks the night,
  But Thou beam'st brightly on.
She only shines with borrowed light,   55
  But Thine is all Thine Own!

Lines

We leave our bodies in the Tomb,
 Like dust to moulder and decay,
But, while they waste in coffined gloom,
 Our parted spirits, where are they?
 In endless night or endless day?   5
Buried as our bodies are
Beyond all earthly hope or fear?
Like them no more to reappear,
 But festering fast away?
For future's but the shadow thrown   10
From present and, the substance gone,
 Its shadow cannot stay!

Memory

Memory! how thy magic fingers,
 With a wild and passing thrill,
Wake the chord whose spirit lingers,
 Sleeping silently and still,

Fast asleep and almost dying,   5
 Through my days of changeless pain,
Till I deem those strings are lying,
 Never to be waked again.

Winds have blown, but all unknown;
Nothing could arouse a tone   10
In that heart which like a stone
 Senselessly has lain.

All seemed over – friend and lover
 Strove to waken music there;

Flow the strings their fingers over,   15
   Still in silence slept the air.

Memory! Memory comes at last,
Memory of feelings past,
And with an Æolian blast
   Strikes the strings resistlessly.   20

'Oh, all our cares'

Oh, all our cares these noontide airs
   Might seem to drive away,
So glad and bright each sight appears,
   Each sound so soft and gay;
And through the shade of yonder glade,   5
   Where thick the leaves are dancing,
While jewels rare and flow'rets fair
   A hundred plumes are glancing.
For there the palace portals rise
   Beyond the myrtle grove,   10
Catching the whitest, brightest dyes
   From the deep blue dome above.
But here this little lonely spot,
   Retires among its trees,
By all unknown and noticed not,   15
   Save sunshine and the breeze.

'The man who will not know another'

The man who will not know another,
 Whose heart can never sympathise,
Who loves not comrade, friend, or brother,
 Unhonoured lives – unnoticed dies:
His frozen eye, his bloodless heart,   5
Nature, repugnant, bids depart.

O Grundy, born for nobler aim,
Be thine the task to shun such shame;
And henceforth never think that he
Who gives his hand in courtesy   10
To one who kindly feels to him,
His gentle birth or name can dim.

However mean a man may be,
Know man *is* man as well as thee;
However high thy gentle line,   15
Know he who writes can rank with thine;
And though his frame be worn and dead,
Some light still glitters round his head.

Yes! though his tottering limbs seem old,
His heart and blood are not yet cold.   20
Ah, Grundy! shun his evil ways,
His restless nights, his troubled days;
But never slight his mind, which flies,
Instinct with noble sympathies,
Afar from spleen and treachery,   25
To thought, to kindness, and to thee.

On Caroline

The light of thy ancestral hall,
   Thy Caroline, no longer smiles:
She has changed her palace for a pall,
   Her garden walks for minster aisles:
Eternal sleep has stilled her breast   5
   Where peace and pleasure made their shrine;
Her golden head has sunk to rest –
   Oh, would that rest made calmer mine!

To thee, while watching o'er the bed
   Where, mute and motionless, she lay,   10
How slow the midnight moments sped!
   How void of sunlight woke the day!
Nor ope'd her eyes to morning's beam,
   Though all around thee woke to her;
Nor broke thy raven-pinioned dream   15
   Of coffin, shroud, and sepulchre.

Why beats thy breast when hers is still?
   Why linger'st thou when she is gone?
Hop'st thou to light on good or ill?
   To find companionship alone?   20
Perhaps thou think'st the churchyard stone
   Can hide past smiles and bury sighs:
That Memory, with her soul, has flown;
   That thou can'st leave her where she lies.

No! joy *itself* is but a shade,   25
   So well may its remembrance die;
But cares, life's conquerors, never fade,
   So strong is their reality!
Thou may'st forget the day which gave
   That child of beauty to thy side,   30
But not the moment when the grave
   Took back again thy borrowed bride.

'Now – but one moment, let me stay'

Now – but one moment, let me stay:
   One moment, ere I go
To join the ranks whose Bugles play
   On Evesham's woody brow.

One calm hour on the brink of life   5
Before I dash amid the strife
   That sounds upon my ear;
That sullen sound whose sullen roll
Bursts over many a parting soul –
   That deep-mouthed voice of war!   10

Here am I standing lonely 'neath
   The shade of quiet trees,
That scarce can catch a single breath
   Of this sweet evening breeze.

And nothing in the twilight sky   15
Except its veil of clouds on high,
   All sleeping calm and grey;
And nothing on the summer gale
But the sweet trumpet's solemn wail
   Slow sounding far away.   20

That and the strange, uncertain sound
   Scarce heard, yet heard by all;
A trembling through the summer ground,
   A murmuring round the wall.

Death Triumphant

Oh! on this first bright Mayday morn,
   That seems to change our earth to Heaven,
May my own bitter thoughts be borne,
   With the wild winter it has driven!
Like this earth, may my mind be made   5
   To feel the freshness round me spreading;
   No other aid to rouse it needing
Than thy glad light, so long delayed.
   Sweet woodland sunshine! – none but thee
   Can wake the joys of memory,   10
Which seemed decaying, as all decayed.

Oh! may they bud, as thou dost now,
   With promise of a summer near!
Nay – let me feel my weary brow –
   Where are the ringlets wreathing there?   15
Why does the hand that shades it tremble?
   Why do these limbs, so languid, shun
   Their walk beneath the morning sun?
Ah, mortal Self! couldst thou dissemble
   Like Sister-Soul! But forms refuse   20
   The real and unreal to confuse.
But, with caprice of fancy, She
Joins things long past with things to be,
Till even I doubt if I have told
   My tale of woes and wonders o'er,   25
Or think Her magic can unfold
   A phantom path of joys before –
Or, laid beneath this Mayday blaze –
Ask, 'Live I o'er departed days?'
Am I the child by Gambia's side,   30
Beneath its woodlands waving wide?
Have I the footsteps bounding free,
The happy laugh of infancy?

To Sestius

Rough winter melts beneath the breeze of spring,
   Nor shun refitted ships the silenced sea,
Nor man nor beasts to folds or firesides cling,
   Nor hoar frosts whiten over field and tree;
   But rising moons each balmy evening, see   5
Fair Venus with her Nymphs and Graces join,
   In merry dances tripping o'er the lea;
While Vulcan makes his roaring furnace shine,
And bids his Cyclops arms in sinewy strength combine.

Now let us, cheerful, crown our heads with flowers,   10
   Spring's first fruits, offered to the newborn year,
And sacrifice beneath the budding bowers,
   A lamb, or kid as Faunus may prefer:
   But – pallid Death, an equal visitor,
Knocks at the poor man's hut, the monarch's tower;   15
   And the few years we have to linger here
Forbid vain dreams of happiness and power,
Beyond what man can crowd into life's fleeting hour.

Soon shall the night that knows no morning come,
   And the dim shades that haunt the eternal shore;   20
And Pluto's shadowy kingdom of the tomb,
   Where Thee the well thrown dice may never more
   Make monarch, while thy friends the wine cup pour;
Where never thou mayest woo fair Lycidas,
   Whose loveliness our ardent youth adore;   25
Whose faultless limbs all other forms surpass,
And, lost amid whose beams, unseen all others pass.

'Oh Thou, whose beams
were most withdrawn'

Oh Thou, whose beams were most withdrawn
   When should have risen my morning sun,
Who, frowning most at earliest dawn,
   Foretold the storms through which 'twould run;

Great God! when hour on hour has passed   5
   In an unsmiling storm away,
No sound but bleak December's blast,
   No sights but tempests, through my day,

At length, in twilight's dark decline,
   Roll back the clouds that mark Thy frown,   10
Give but a single silver line –
   One sunblink, as that day goes down.

My prayer is earnest, for my breast
   No more can buffet with these storms;
I must have one short space of rest   15
   Ere I go home to dust and worms;

I must a single gleam of light
   Amid increasing darkness see,
Ere I, resigned to churchyard night,
   Bid day farewell eternally!   20

My body is oppressed with pain,
   My mind is prostrate 'neath despair –
Nor mind nor body may again
   Do more than call Thy wrath to spare.

Both void of power to fight or flee,   25
   To bear or to avert Thy eye,
With sunken heart, with suppliant knee,
   Implore a peaceful hour to die.

When I look back on former life,
   I scarcely know what I have been,   30
So swift the change from strife to strife
    That passes o'er the 'wildering scene.

I only feel that every power –
    And Thou hadst given much to me –
Was spent upon the present hour,   35
    Was never turned, my God, to Thee;

That what I did to make me blest
    Sooner or later changed to pain;
That still I laughed at peace and rest,
    So neither must behold again.   40

'O God! while I in pleasure's wiles'

O God! while I in pleasure's wiles
    Count hours and years as one,
And deem that, wrapt in pleasure's smiles,
    My joys can ne'er be done,

Give me the stern sustaining power   5
    To look into the past,
And see the darkly shadowed hour
    Which I must meet at last;

The hour when I must stretch this hand
    To give a last adieu   10
To those sad friends that round me stand,
    Whom I no more must view.

For false though bright the hours that lead
    My present passage on,
And when I join the silent dead   15
    Their light will all be gone.

    Then I must cease to seek the light
       Which fires the evening heaven,
    Since to direct through death's dark night
       Some other must be given.   20

Peaceful Death and Painful Life

Why dost thou sorrow for the happy dead?
   For if their life be lost, their toils are o'er
   And woe and want shall trouble them no more.
Nor ever slept they in an earthly bed
So sound as now they sleep while, dreamless, laid   5
   In the dark chambers of that unknown shore
   Where Night and Silence seal each guarded door:
So, turn from such as these thy drooping head
And mourn the 'Dead alive' whose spirit flies –
   Whose life departs before his death has come –   10
Who finds no Heaven beyond Life's gloomy skies,
   Who sees no Hope to brighten up that gloom,
'Tis HE who feels the worm that never dies –
   The REAL death and darkness of the tomb.

Thorp Green

    I sit, this evening, far away
       From all I used to know,
    And nought reminds my soul today
       Of happy long ago.

    Unwelcome cares, unthought-of fears,   5
       Around my room arise;

I seek for suns of former years,
  But clouds o'ercast my skies.

Yes – Memory, wherefore does thy voice
  Bring old times back to view,   10
As thou wouldst bid me not rejoice
  In thoughts and prospects new?

I'll thank thee, Memory, in the hour
  When troubled thoughts are mine –
For thou, like suns in April's shower,   15
  On shadowy scenes wilt shine.

I'll thank thee when approaching death
  Would quench life's feeble ember,
For thou wouldst even renew my breath
  With thy sweet word 'Remember'!   20

Penmænmawr

These winds, these clouds, this chill November storm
Bring back again thy tempest-beaten form
To eyes that look upon yon dreary sky
As late they looked on thy sublimity;
When I, more troubled than thy restless sea,   5
Found, in its waves, companionship with thee.
'Mid mists thou frownedst over Arvon's shore,
'Mid tears I watched thee over ocean's roar,
And thy blue front, by thousand storms laid bare,
Claimed kindred with a heart worn down by care.   10
No smile had'st thou, o'er smiling fields aspiring,
And none had I, from smiling fields retiring;
Blackness, 'mid sunlight, tinged thy slaty brow,
I, 'mid sweet music, looked as dark as thou;
Old Scotland's song, o'er murmuring surges borne, 15
Of 'times departed, – never to return,'
Was echoed back in mournful tones from thee,
And found an echo, quite as sad, in me;

Waves, clouds, and shadows moved in restless change,
Around, above, and on thy rocky range,   20
But seldom saw that sovereign front of thine
Changes more quick than those which passed o'er mine.
And as wild winds and human hands, at length,
Have turned to scattered stones the mighty strength
Of that old fort, whose belt of boulders grey   25
Roman or Saxon legions held at bay;
So had, methought, the young, unshaken nerve –
That, when WILL wished, no doubt could cause to swerve,
That on its vigour ever placed reliance,
That to its sorrows sometimes bade defiance –   30
Now left my spirit, like thyself, old hill,
With head defenceless against human ill;
And, as thou long hast looked upon the wave
That takes, but gives not, like a churchyard grave,
I, like life's course, through ether's weary range,   35
Never know rest from ceaseless strife and change.

But, PENMÆNMAWR! a better fate was thine,
Through all its shades, than that which darkened mine:
No quick thoughts thrilled through thy gigantic mass
Of woe for what might be, or is, or was;   40
Thou hadst no memory of the glorious hour
When Britain rested on thy giant power;
Thou hadst no feeling for the verdant slope
That leant on thee as man's heart leans on hope;
The pastures, chequered o'er with cot and tree,   45
Though thou wert guardian, got no smile from thee;
Old ocean's wrath their charm might overwhelm,
But thou could'st still keep thy unshaken realm –
While I felt flashes of an inward feeling
As fierce as those thy craggy form revealing   50
In nights of blinding gleams, when deafening roar
Hurls back thy echo to old Mona's shore.
I knew a flower, whose leaves were meant to bloom
'Till Death should snatch it to adorn a tomb,
Now, blanching 'neath the blight of hopeless grief,   55

With never blooming, and yet living leaf;
A flower on which my mind would wish to shine,
If but one beam could break from mind like mine.
I had an ear which could on accents dwell
That might as well say 'perish!' as 'farewell!'   . 60
An eye which saw, far off, a tender form,
Beaten, unsheltered, by affliction's storm;
An arm – a lip – that trembled to embrace
My angel's gentle breast and sorrowing face,
A mind that clung to Ouse's fertile side   65
While tossing – objectless – on Menai's tide!

Oh, Soul! that draw'st yon mighty hill and me
Into communion of vague unity,
Tell me, can I obtain the stony brow
That fronts the storm, as much unbroken now   70
As when it once upheld the fortress proud,
Now gone, like its own morning cap of cloud?
Its breast is stone. Can I have one of steel,
To endure – inflict – defend – yet never feel?
It stood as firm when haughty Edward's word   75
Gave hill and dale to England's fire and sword,
As when white sails and steam-smoke tracked the sea,
And all the world breathed peace, but waves and me.

Let me, like it, arise o'er mortal care,
All woes sustain, yet never know despair;   80
Unshrinking face the grief I now deplore,
And stand, through storm and shine, like moveless
      PENMÆNMAWR!

Epistle From a Father to a Child in Her Grave

From Earth, – whose life-reviving April showers
Hide withered grass 'neath Springtide's herald flowers,
And give, in each soft wind that drives her rain,
Promise of fields and forests rich again, –
I write to thee, the aspect of whose face   5
Can never change with altered time or place;
Whose eyes could look on India's fiercest wars
Less shrinking than the boldest son of Mars;
Whose lips, more firm than Stoic's long ago,
Would neither smile with joy nor blanch with woe;   10
Whose limbs could sufferings far more firmly bear
Than mightiest heroes in the storms of war;
Whose frame, nor wishes good, nor shrinks from ill,
Nor feels distraction's throb, nor pleasure's thrill.

  I write to thee what thou wilt never read,   15
For heed me thou *will not*, howe'er may bleed
The heart that many think a worthless stone,
But which oft aches for some beloved one;
Nor, if that life, mysterious, from on high,
Once more gave feeling to thy stony eye,   20
Could'st thou thy father know, or feel that he
Gave life and lineaments and thoughts to thee;
For when thou died'st, thy day was in its dawn,
And night still struggled with Life's opening morn;
The twilight star of childhood, thy young days   25
Alone illumined, with its twinkling rays,
So sweet, yet feeble, given from those dusk skies.
Whose kindling, coming noontide prophesies.
But tells us not that Summer's noon can shroud
Our sunshine with a veil of thundercloud.   30

If, when thou freely gave the life, that ne'er
To thee had given either hope or fear,
But quietly had shone; nor asked if joy
Thy future course should cheer, or grief annoy;

If then thoud'st seen, upon a summer sea,   35
One, once in features, as in blood, like thee,
On skies of azure blue and waters green,
Melting to mist amid the summer sheen,
In trouble gazing – ever hesitating
'Twixt miseries each hour new dread creating,   40
And joys – whate'er they cost – still doubly dear,
Those 'troubled pleasures soon chastised by fear;'
If thou *had'st* seen him, thou would'st ne'er believe
That thou had'st yet known what it was to live!

Thine eyes could only see thy mother's breast;   45
Thy feelings only wished on that to rest;
That was thy world; – thy food and sleep it gave,
And slight the change 'twixt it and childhood's grave.
Thou saw'st this world like one who, prone, reposes,
Upon a plain, and in a bed of roses,   50
With nought in sight save marbled skies above,
Nought heard but breezes whispering in the grove:
I – thy life's source – was like a wanderer breasting
Keen mountain winds, and on a summit resting,
Whose rough rocks rose above the grassy mead,   55
With sleet and north winds howling overhead,
And Nature, like a map, beneath him spread;
Far winding river, tree, and tower, and town,
Shadow and sunlight, 'neath his gaze marked down
By that mysterious hand which graves the plan   60
Of that drear country called 'The Life of Man.'

If seen, men's eyes would loathing shrink from thee,
And turn, perhaps, with no disgust to me;
Yet thou had'st beauty, innocence, and smiles,
And now hast rest from this world's woes and wiles,   65
While I have restlessness and worrying care,
So sure, thy lot is brighter, happier far.

   So let it be; and though thy ears may never
Hear these lines read beyond Death's darksome river,
Not vainly from the borders of despair   70
May rise a sound of joy that thou art freed from care!

Emily Jane Brontë

'Will the day be bright or cloudy?'

Will the day be bright or cloudy?
Sweetly has its dawn begun,
But the heaven may shake with thunder
Ere the setting of the sun.

Lady, watch Apollo's journey,   5
Thus thy firstborn's course shall be –
If his beams through summer vapours
Warm the earth all placidly,
Her days shall pass like a pleasant dream in sweet tranquillity.

If it darken, if a shadow   10
Quench his rays and summon rain,
Flowers may open, buds may blossom,
Bud and flower alike are vain;
Her days shall pass like a mournful story in care and tears and
      pain.

If the wind be fresh and free,   15
The wide skies clear and cloudless blue,
The woods and fields and golden flowers
Sparkling in sunshine and in dew,
Her days shall pass in Glory's light the world's drear desert
      through.

'Tell me, tell me, smiling child'

Tell me, tell me, smiling child,
What the past is like to thee?
An Autumn evening soft and mild
With a wind that sighs mournfully.

Tell me what is the present hour?   5
A green and flowery spray
Where a young bird sits gathering its power
To mount and fly away.

And what is the future, happy one?
A sea beneath a cloudless sun,   10
A mighty glorious dazzling sea
Stretching into infinity.

'Alone I sat'

Alone I sat, the summer day
Had died in smiling light away;
I saw it die, I watched it fade
From misty hill and breezeless glade,

And thoughts in my soul were rushing   5
And my heart bowed beneath their power,
And tears within my eyes were gushing
Because I could not speak the feeling.
The solemn joy around me stealing
In that divine untroubled hour.   10

I asked my self, O why has heaven
Denied the precious gift to me,
The glorious gift to many given
To speak their thoughts in poetry?

Dreams have encircled me, I said,   15
From careless childhood's sunny time,
Visions by ardent fancy fed
Since life was in its morning prime.

But now when I had hoped to sing
My fingers strike a tuneless string   20
And still the burden of the strain
Is: Strive no more, 'tis all in vain.

Lines

Far away is the land of rest,
Thousand miles are stretched between;
Many a mountain's stormy crest,
Many a desert void of green.

Wasted worn is the traveller,   5
Dark his heart and dim his eye,
Without hope or comforter
Faltering faint and ready to die.

Often he looks to the ruthless sky,
Often he looks o'er his dreary road,   10
Often he wishes down to lie
And render up life's tiresome load.

But yet faint not. mournful man,
Leagues on leagues are left behind
Since your sunless course began.   15
Then go on to toil resigned.

If you still despair control,
Hush its whispers in your breast;
You shall reach the final goal,
You shall win the land of rest.   20

Lines

I die, but when the grave shall press
The heart so long endeared to thee –
When earthly cares no more distress
And earthly joys are nought to me,

Weep not, but think that I have past   5
Before thee o'er a sea of gloom,
Have anchored safe and rest at last
Where tears and mourning cannot come.

'Tis I should weep to leave thee here
On that dark Ocean sailing drear,   10
With storms around and fears before
And no kind light to point the shore.

But long or short though life may be
'Tis nothing to eternity.
We part below to meet on high   15
Where blissful ages never die.

To a Wreath of Snow
by A. G. Almeda

O transient voyager of heaven!
O silent sign of winter skies!
What adverse wind thy sail has driven
To dungeons where a prisoner lies?

Methinks the hands that shut the sun   5
So sternly from this mourning brow
Might still their rebel task have done,
And checked a thing so frail as thou.

They would have done it had they known
The talisman that dwelt in thee,   10
For all the suns that ever shone
Have never been so kind to me!

For many a week, and many a day,
My heart was weighed with sinking gloom
When morning rose, in mourning grey,   15
And faintly lit my prison room,

But angel-like, when I awoke,
Thy silvery form so soft and fair
Shining through darkness, sweetly spoke
Of cloudy skies and mountains bare,   20

The dearest to a mountaineer,
Who, all life long has loved the snow
That crowned her native summits drear,
Better, than greenest plains below –

And voiceless, soulless, messenger   25
Thy presence waked a thrilling tone
That comforts me while thou art here
And will sustain when thou art gone.

Song to A. A.

This shall be thy lullaby
Rocking on the stormy sea,
Though it roar in thunder wild
Sleep – stilly sleep – my dark-haired child.

When our shuddering boat was crossing   5
Elderno lake so rudely tossing.
Then 'twas first my nursling smiled;
Sleep – softly sleep – my fairbrowed child.

Waves above thy cradle break,
Foamy tears are on thy cheek,   10
Yet the ocean's self grows mild
When it bears my slumbering child.

Song by Julius Brenzaida
to G. S.

Geraldine, the moon is shining
With so soft, so bright a ray,
Seems it not that eve, declining,
Ushered in a fairer day?

While the wind is whispering only,   5
Far – across the water borne,
Let us, in this silence lonely
Sit beneath the ancient thorn.

Wild the road, and rough and dreary;
Barren all the moorland round;   10
Rude the couch that rests us weary;
Mossy stone and heathy ground –

But when winter storms were meeting
In the moonless midnight dome.
Did we heed the tempest's beating   15
Howling round our spirits' home?

No, that tree, with branches riven
Whitening in the whirl of snow,
As it tossed against the heaven,
Sheltered happy hearts below –   20

And at Autumn's mild returning
Shall our feet forget the way?

And in Cynthia's silver morning,
Geraldine, wilt thou delay?

F. De Samara to A. G. A.

Light up thy halls! 'Tis closing day;
I'm drear and lone and far away –
Cold blows on my breast, and northwind's bitter sigh
And oh, my couch is bleak beneath the rainy sky!

Light up thy halls – and think not of me;   5
That face is absent now, thou has hated so to see –
Bright be thine eyes, undimmed their dazzling shine,
For never, never more shall they encounter mine!

The desert moor is dark; there is tempest in the air:
I have breathed my only wish in one last, one burning prayer – 10
A prayer that would come forth although it lingered long:
That set on fire my heart, but froze upon my tongue –

And now, it shall be done before the morning rise;
I will not watch the sun ascend in yonder skies.
One task alone remains – thy pictured face to view   15
And then I go to prove if God, at least, be true!

Do I not see thee now? Thy black resplendent hair;
Thy glory-beaming brow, and smile how heavenly fair!
Thine eyes are turned away – those eyes I would not see:
Their dark, their deadly ray would more than madden me.   20

There, go, Deceiver, go! my hand is streaming wet;
My heart's blood flows to buy the blessing – To forget!
Oh could that lost heart give back, back again to thine
One tenth part of the pain that clouds my dark decline!

Oh could I see thy lids weighed down in cheerless woe;   25
Too full to hide their tears, too stern to overflow;
Oh could I know thy soul with equal grief was torn –
This fate might be endured – this anguish might be borne!

How gloomy grows the Night! 'Tis Gondal's wind that blows.
I shall not tread again the deep glens where it rose –   30
I feel it on my face – where, wild Blast, dost thou roam?
What do we, wanderer, here? So far away from home?

I do not need thy breath to cool my death-cold brow,
But go to that far land where She is shining now;
Tell Her my latest wish, tell Her my dreary doom;   35
Say, that *my* pangs are past, but *Hers* are yet to come –

Vain words – vain, frenzied thoughts! No ear can hear me call –
Lost in the vacant air my frantic curses fall –
And could she see me now, perchance her lip would smile,
Would smile in careless pride and utter scorn the while!   40

And yet, for all Her hate, each parting glance would tell
A stronger passion breathed, burned in this last farewell –
Unconquered in my soul the Tyrant rules me still –
Life bows to my control, but, *Love* I cannot kill!

'Loud without the wind was roaring'

Loud without the wind was roaring
    Through the waned autumnal sky,
Drenching wet, the cold rain pouring
    Spoke of stormy winters nigh.

    All too like that dreary eve   5
    Sighed within repining grief –
    Sighed at first – but sighed not long
    Sweet – How softly sweet it came!

Wild words of an ancient song –
Undefined, without a name –   10

'It was spring, for the skylark was singing.'
Those words they awakened a spell –
They unlocked a deep fountain whose springing
Nor Absence nor Distance can quell.

In the gloom of a cloudy November   15
They uttered the music of May –
They kindled the perishing ember
Into fervour that could not decay.

Awaken on all my dear moorlands
The wind in its glory and pride!   20
O call me from valleys and highlands
To walk by the hill-river's side!

It swelled with the first snowy weather;
The rocks they are icy and hoar
And darker waves round the long heather   25
And the fern-leaves are sunny no more.

There are no yellow-stars on the mountain,
The blue-bells have long died away
From the brink of the moss-bedded fountain,
From the side of the wintery brae –   30

But lovelier than corn-fields all waving
In emerald and scarlet and gold
Are the slopes where the north-wind is raving
And the glens where I wandered of old –

'It was morning, the bright sun was beaming.'   35
How sweetly that brought back to me
The time when nor labour nor dreaming
Broke the sleep of the happy and free.

But blithely we rose as the dusk heaven
Was melting to amber and blue   40

And swift were the wings to our feet given
While we traversed the meadows of dew.

For the moors, for the moors where the short grass
Like velvet beneath us should lie!
For the moors, for the moors where each high pass   45
Rose sunny against the clear sky!

For the moors, where the linnet was trilling
Its song on the old granite stone –
Where the lark – the wild sky-lark was filling
Every breast with delight like its own.   50

What language can utter the feeling
That rose when, in exile afar,
On the brow of a lonely hill kneeling
I saw the brown heath growing there.

It was scattered and stunted, and told me   55
That soon even that would be gone;
It whispered, 'The grim walls enfold me,
I have bloomed in my last summer's sun.'

But not the loved music whose waking
Makes the soul of the Swiss die away   60
Has a spell more adored and heart-breaking
Than in its half-blighted bells lay–

The spirit that bent 'neath its power
How it longed, how it burned to be free!
If I could have wept in that hour   65
Those tears had been heaven to me –

Well, well the sad minutes are moving
Though loaded with trouble and pain –
And sometime the loved and the loving
Shall meet on the mountains again –   70

'The blue bell is the sweetest flower'

The blue bell is the sweetest flower
That waves in summer air;
Its blossoms have the mightiest power
To soothe my spirit's care.

There is a spell in purple heath   5
Too wildly, sadly drear;
The violet has a fragrant breath
But fragrance will not cheer.

The trees are bare, the sun is cold
And seldom, seldom seen –   10
The heavens have lost their zone of gold,
The earth its robe of green,

And ice upon the glancing stream
Has cast its sombre shade,
And distant hills and valleys seem   15
In frozen mist arrayed –

The blue bell cannot charm me now,
The heath has lost its bloom,
The violets in the glen below
They yield no sweet perfume.   20

But though I mourn the heather-bell,
'Tis better far away;
I know how fast my tears would swell
To see it smile today.

And that wood flower that hides so shy   25
Beneath the mossy stone
Its balmy scent and dewy eye –
'Tis not for them I moan.

It is the slight and stately stem,
The blossom's silvery blue.   30

The buds hid like a sapphire gem
In sheaths of emerald hue.

'Tis these that breathe upon my heart
A calm and softening spell
That if it makes the tear-drop start   35
Has power to soothe as well.

For these I weep. so long divided
Through winter's dreary day,
In longing weep – but most when guided
On withered banks to stray;   40

If chilly then the light should fall
Adown the dreary sky
And gild the dank and darkened wall
With transient brilliancy,

How do I yearn, how do I pine   45
For the time of flowers to come,
And turn me from that fading shine –
To mourn the fields of home –

Song

King Julius left the south country,
His banners all bravely flying,
His followers went out with Jubilee,
But they shall return with sighing.

Loud arose the triumphal hymn,   5
The drums were loudly rolling,
Yet you might have heard in distance dim
How a passing-bell was tolling.

The sword so bright from battles won
With unseen rust is fretting,   10
The evening comes before the noon,
The scarce risen sun is setting.

While princes hang upon his breath
And nations round are fearing,
Close by his side a daggered Death   15
With sheathless point stands sneering.

That death he took a certain aim,
For Death is stony-hearted,
And in the zenith of his fame
Both power and life departed.   20

'Come hither, child'

Come hither, child – who gifted thee
With power to touch that string so well?
How daredst thou rouse up thoughts in me,
Thoughts that I would – but cannot quell?

Nay chide not, lady, long ago   5
I heard those notes in Ula's hall
And had I known they'd waken woe
I'd weep their music to recall.

But thus it was, one festal night
When I was hardly six years old,   10
I stole away from crowds and light
And sought a chamber dark and cold.

I had no one to love me there,
I knew no comrade and no friend,
And so I went to sorrow where   15
Heaven, only heaven, saw me bend.

Loud blew the wind, 'twas sad to stay
From all that splendour barred away;
I imaged in the lonely room
A thousand forms of fearful gloom   20

And with my wet eyes raised on high
I prayed to God that I might die.
Suddenly in that silence drear
A sound of music reached my ear.

And then a note, I hear it yet,   25
So full of soul, so deeply sweet
I thought that Gabriel's self had come
To take me to my father's home.

Three times it rose, that seraph-strain,
Then died nor lived ever again,   30
But still the words and still the tone
Swell round my heart when all alone.

Song

O between distress and pleasure
Fond affection cannot be,
Wretched hearts in vain would treasure
Friendship's joys when others flee.

Well I know thine eye would never   5
Smile when mine grieved willingly,
Yet I know thine eye forever
Could not weep in sympathy.

Let us part, the time is over
When I thought and felt like thee.   10
I will be an Ocean rover,
I will sail the desert sea.

Isles there are beyond its billow,
Lands where woe may wander free,
And, beloved, thy midnight pillow   15
Will be soft unwatched by me.

Not on each returning morrow
When thy heart bounds ardently
Needst thou then dissemble sorrow,
Marking my despondency.   20

Day by day some dreary token
Will forsake thy memory,
Till at last all old links broken,
I shall be a dream to thee.

'Love is like the wild rose briar'

Love is like the wild rose briar,
Friendship, like the holly tree,
The holly is dark when the rose briar blooms,
But which will bloom most constantly?

The wild rose briar is sweet in spring,   5
Its summer blossoms scent the air;
Yet wait till winter comes again
And who will call the wild-briar fair?

Then scorn the silly rose-wreath now
And deck thee with the holly's sheen,   10
That when December blights thy brow
He still may leave thy garland green –

'Come, walk with me'

Come, walk with me,
There's only thee
To bless my spirit now –
We used to love on winter nights
To wander through the snow;   5
Can we not woo back old delights?
The clouds rush dark and wild,
They fleck with shade our mountain heights,
The same as long ago,
And on the horizon rest at last   10
In looming masses piled;
While moonbeams flash and fly so fast
We scarce can say they smiled.

Come walk with me, come walk with me;
We were not once so few,   15
But Death has stolen our company
As sunshine steals the dew –
He took them one by one and we
Are left – the only two;
So closer would my feelings twine   20
Because they have no stay but thine –

'Nay call me not – it may not be,
Is human love so true?
Can Friendship's flower droop on for years
And then revive anew?   25
No, though the soil be wet with tears,
How fair so e'er it grew
The vital sap once perished
Will never flow again,
And surer than that dwelling dread,   30
The narrow dungeon of the Dead,
Time parts the hearts of men –'

Stanzas

I'll not weep that thou art going to leave me,
  There's nothing lovely here;
And doubly will the dark world grieve me,
  While thy heart suffers there.

I'll not weep, because the summer's glory   5
  Must always end in gloom;
And, follow out the happiest story –
  It closes with a tomb!

And I am weary of the anguish
  Increasing winters bear;   10
Weary to watch the spirit languish
  Through years of dead despair.

So, if a tear, when thou art dying,
  Should haply fall from me,
It is but that my soul is sighing,   15
  To go and rest with thee.

'If grief for grief can touch thee'

If grief for grief can touch thee,
If answering woe for woe,
If any ruth can melt thee
Come to me now!

I cannot be more lonely,   5
More drear I cannot be!
My worn heart throbs so wildly
'Twill break for thee –

And when the world despises –
When Heaven repels my prayer –   10
Will not mine angel comfort?
Mine idol hear?

Yes, by the tears I've poured,
By all my hours of pain,
O I shall surely win thee   15
Beloved, again!

The Night-Wind

In summer's mellow midnight
A cloudless moon shone through
Our open parlour window
And rosetrees wet with dew –

I sat in silent musing –   5
    The soft wind waved my hair,
It told me Heaven was glorious
And sleeping Earth was fair –

I needed not its breathing
To bring such thoughts to me,   10
But still it whispered lowly,
'How dark the woods will be! –

'The thick leaves in my murmur
Are rustling like a dream,
And all their myriad voices   15
Instinct with spirit seem.'

I said, 'Go, gentle singer,
Thy wooing voice is kind
But do not think its music
Has power to reach my mind –   20

'Play with the scented flower,
The young tree's supple bough –
And leave my human feelings
In their own course to flow.'

The Wanderer would not leave me,   25
Its kiss grew warmer still –
'O come,' it sighed so sweetly,
'I'll win thee 'gainst thy will –

'Have we not been from childhood friends?
Have I not loved thee long?   30
As long as thou hast loved the night
Whose silence wakes my song?

'And when thy heart is laid at rest
Beneath the church-yard stone
I shall have time enough to mourn   35
And thou to be alone –'

The Old Stoic

Riches I hold in light esteem;
    And Love I laugh to scorn;
And lust of fame was but a dream
    That vanished with the morn:

And if I pray, the only prayer   5
    That moves my lips for me
Is, 'Leave the heart that now I bear,
    And give me liberty!'

Yes, as my swift days near their goal,
    'Tis all that I implore;   10
In life and death, a chainless soul,
    With courage to endure.

To A. G. A.

'Thou standest in the green-wood now
The place, the hour, the same –
And here the fresh leaves gleam and glow,
And there, down in the lake below,
The tiny ripples flame –   5

'The breeze sings like a summer breeze
Should sing in summer skies,
And tower-like rocks and tent-like trees
In mingled glory rise.

'But where is he today, today?'   10
'O question not with me –'
'I will not, Lady, only say
Where may thy lover be? –

'Is he upon some distant shore?
Or is he on the sea?   15
Or is the heart thou dost adore
A faithless heart to thee?'

'The heart I love, whate'er betide
Is faithful as the grave,
And neither foreign lands divide   20
Nor yet the rolling wave –'

'Then why should sorrow cloud that brow,
And tears those eyes bedim?
Reply this once, is it that thou
Hast faithless been to him?'   25

'I gazed upon the cloudless moon
And loved her all the night
Till morning came and ardent noon
Then I forgot her light –

'No – not forgot, eternally   30
Remains its memory dear;
But could the day seem dark to me
Because the night was fair?

'I well may mourn that only one
Can light my future sky,   35
Even though by such a radiant sun
My moon of life must die –'

Hope

Hope was but a timid friend;
    She sat without the grated den,
Watching how my fate would tend,
    Even as selfish-hearted men.

She was cruel in her fear;   5
    Through the bars, one dreary day,
I looked out to see her there,
    And she turned her face away!

Like a false guard, false watch keeping,
    Still, in strife, she whispered peace;   10
She would sing while I was weeping;
    If I listened, she would cease.

False she was, and unrelenting;
    When my last joys strewed the ground,
Even Sorrow saw, repenting,   15
    Those sad relics scattered round;

Hope, whose whisper would have given
    Balm to all my frenzied pain,
Stretched her wings, and soared to heaven,
    Went, and ne'er returned again!   20

Song

The linnet in the rocky dells,
  The moor-lark in the air,
The bee among the heather bells,
  That hide my lady fair:

The wild deer browse above her breast;   5
  The wild birds raise their brood;
And they, her smiles of love caressed,
  Have left her solitude!

I ween, that when the grave's dark wall
  Did first her form retain;   10
They thought their hearts could ne'er recall
  The light of joy again.

They thought the tide of grief would flow
  Unchecked through future years;
But where is all their anguish now,   15
  And where are all their tears?

Well, let them fight for honour's breath,
  Or pleasure's shade pursue –
The dweller in the land of death
  Is changed and careless too.   20

And, if their eyes should watch and weep
  Till sorrow's source were dry,
She would not, in her tranquil sleep,
  Return a single sigh!

Blow, west-wind, by the lonely mound,   25
  And murmur, summer-streams –
There is no need of other sound
  To soothe my lady's dreams.

To Imagination

When weary with the long day's care,
   And earthly change from pain to pain,
And lost and ready to despair,
   Thy kind voice calls me back again:
Oh, my true friend! I am not lone,   5
While thou canst speak with such a tone!

So hopeless is the world without;
   The world within I doubly prize;
Thy world, where guile, and hate, and doubt,
   And cold suspicion never rise;   10
Where thou, and I, and Liberty,
Have undisputed sovereignty.

What matters it, that, all around,
   Danger, and guilt, and darkness lie,
If but within our bosom's bound   15
   We hold a bright, untroubled sky,
Warm with ten thousand mingled rays
Of suns that know no winter days?

Reason, indeed, may oft complain
   For Nature's sad reality,   20
And tell the suffering heart, how vain
   Its cherished dreams must always be;
And Truth may rudely trample down
The flowers of Fancy, newly-blown:

But, thou art ever there, to bring   25
   The hovering vision back, and breathe
New glories o'er the blighted spring,
   And call a lovelier Life from Death,
And whisper, with a voice divine,
Of real worlds, as bright as thine.   30

I trust not to thy phantom bliss,
   Yet, still, in evening's quiet hour,

With never-failing thankfulness,
   I welcome thee, Benignant Power;
Sure solacer of human cares,   35
And sweeter hope, when hope despairs!

A Death-Scene

'O Day! he cannot die
When thou so fair art shining!
O Sun, in such a glorious sky,
So tranquilly declining;

He cannot leave thee now,   5
While fresh west winds are blowing,
And all around his youthful brow
Thy cheerful light is glowing!

Edward, awake, awake –
The golden evening gleams   10
Warm and bright on Arden's lake –
Arouse thee from thy dreams!

Beside thee, on my knee,
My dearest friend! I pray
That thou, to cross the eternal sea,   15
Wouldst yet one hour delay:

I hear its billows roar –
I see them foaming high;
But no glimpse of a further shore
Has blest my straining eye.   20

Believe not what they urge
Of Eden isles beyond;
Turn back, from that tempestuous surge,
To thy own native land.

It is not death, but pain
That struggles in thy breast –
Nay, rally, Edward, rouse again;
I cannot let thee rest!'

One long lock, that sore reproved me
For the woe I could not bear –
One mute look of suffering moved me
To repent my useless prayer:

And, with sudden check, the heaving
Of distraction passed away;
Not a sign of further grieving
Stirred my soul that awful day.

Paled, at length, the sweet sun setting;
Sunk to peace the twilight breeze:
Summer dews fell softly, wetting
Glen, and glade, and silent trees.

Then his eyes began to weary,
Weighed beneath a mortal sleep;
And their orbs grew strangely dreary,
Clouded, even as they would weep.

But they wept not, but they changed not,
Never moved, and never closed;
Troubled still, and still they ranged not –
Wandered not, nor yet reposed!

So I knew that he was dying –
Stooped, and raised his languid head;
Felt no breath, and heard no sighing,
So I knew that he was dead.

Remembrance

Cold in the earth – and the deep snow piled above thee,
Far, far, removed, cold in the dreary grave!
Have I forgot, my only Love, to love thee,
Severed at last by Time's all-severing wave?

Now, when alone, do my thoughts no longer hover   5
Over the mountains, on that northern shore,
Resting their wings where heath and fern-leaves cover
Thy noble heart for ever, ever more?

Cold in the earth – and fifteen wild Decembers,
From those brown hills, have melted into spring: 10
Faithful, indeed, is the spirit that remembers
After such years of change and suffering!

Sweet Love of youth, forgive, if I forget thee,
While the world's tide is bearing me along;
Other desires and other hopes beset me,   15
Hopes which obscure, but cannot do thee wrong!

No later light has lightened up my heaven,
No second morn has ever shone for me;
All my life's bliss from thy dear life was given,
All my life's bliss is in the grave with thee.   20

But, when the days of golden dreams had perished,
And even Despair was powerless to destroy;
Then did I learn how existence could be cherished,
Strengthened, and fed without the aid of joy.

Then did I check the tears of useless passion –   25
Weaned my young soul from yearning after thine;
Sternly denied its burning wish to hasten
Down to that tomb already more than mine.

And, even yet, I dare not let it languish,
Dare not indulge in memory's rapturous pain;   30

Once drinking deep of that divinest anguish,
How could I seek the empty world again?

Death

Death! that struck when I was most confiding
In my certain faith of joy to be –
Strike again, Time's withered branch dividing
From the fresh root of Eternity!

Leaves, upon Time's branch, were growing brightly,   5
Full of sap, and full of silver dew;
Birds beneath its shelter gathered nightly;
Daily round its flowers the wild bees flew.

Sorrow passed, and plucked the golden blossom;
Guilt stripped off the foliage in its pride;   10
But, within its parent's kindly bosom,
Flowed for ever Life's restoring tide.

Little mourned I for the parted gladness,
For the vacant nest and silent song –
Hope was there, and laughed me out of sadness;   15
Whispering, 'Winter will not linger long!'

And, behold! with tenfold increase blessing,
Spring adorned the beauty-burdened spray;
Wind and rain and fervent heat, caressing,
Lavished glory on that second May!   20

High it rose – no winged grief could sweep it;
Sin was scared to distance with its shine;
Love, and its own life, had power to keep it
From all wrong – from every blight but thine!

Cruel Death! The young leaves droop and languish;   25
Evening's gentle air may still restore –

No! the morning sunshine mocks my anguish –
Time, for me, must never blossom more!

Strike it down, that other boughs may flourish
Where that perished sapling used to be;   30
Thus, at least, its mouldering corpse will nourish
That from which it sprung – Eternity.

Stars

Ah! why, because the dazzling sun
   Restored our Earth to joy,
Have you departed, every one,
   And left a desert sky?

All through the night, your glorious eyes   5
   Were gazing down in mine,
And, with a full heart's thankful sighs,
   I blessed that watch divine.

I was at peace, and drank your beams
   As they were life to me;   10
And revelled in my changeful dreams,
   Like petrel on the sea.

Thought followed thought, star followed star,
   Through boundless regions, on;
While one sweet influence, near and far,   15
   Thrilled through, and proved us one!

Why did the morning dawn to break
   So great, so pure, a spell;
And scorch with fire, the tranquil cheek,
   Where your cool radiance fell?   20

Blood-red, he rose, and, arrow-straight,
   His fierce beams struck my brow;
The soul of nature, sprang, elate,
   But *mine* sank sad and low!

My lids closed down, yet through their veil,   25
   I saw him, blazing, still,
And steep in gold the misty dale,
   And flash upon the hill.

I turned me to the pillow, then,
   To call back night, and see   30
Your worlds of solemn light, again,
   Throb with my heart, and me!

It would not do – the pillow glowed,
   And glowed both roof and floor;
And birds sang loudly in the wood,   35
   And fresh winds shook the door;

The curtains waved, the wakened flies
   Were murmuring round my room,
Imprisoned there, till I should rise,
   And give them leave to roam.   40

Oh, stars, and dreams, and gentle night;
   Oh, night and stars return!
And hide me from the hostile light,
   That does not warm, but burn;

That drains the blood of suffering men: 45
   Drinks tears, instead of dew;
Let me sleep through his blinding reign,
   And only wake with you!

A. E. and R. C.

Heavy hangs the raindrop
From the burdened spray;
Heavy broods the damp mist
On Uplands far away;

Heavy looms the dull sky,   5
Heavy rolls the sea –
And heavy beats the young heart
Beneath that lonely tree –

Never has a blue streak
Cleft the clouds since morn –   10
Never has his grim Fate
Smiled since he was born –

Frowning on the infant,
Shadowing childhood's joy;
Guardian angel knows not   15
That melancholy boy.

Day is passing swiftly
Its sad and sombre prime;
Youth is fast invading
Sterner manhood's time –   20

All the flowers are praying
For sun before they close,
And he prays too, unknowing,
That sunless human rose!

Blossoms, that the westwind   25
Has never wooed to blow,
Scentless are your petals,
Your dew as cold as snow.

Soul, where kindred kindness
No early promise woke,   30

Barren is your beauty
As weed upon the rock –

Wither, Brothers, wither,
You were vainly given –
Earth reserves no blessing   35
For the unblessed of Heaven!

Child of Delight! with sunbright hair
And seablue, seadeep eyes,
Spirit of Bliss, what brings thee here
Beneath these sullen skies?   40

Thou shouldest live in eternal spring
Where endless day is never dim,
Why, seraph, has thy erring wing
Borne thee down to weep with him?

'Ah, not from heaven am I descended   45
And I do not come to mingle tears,
But sweet is day, though with shadows blended,
And though clouded, sweet are youthful years –

'I, the image of light and gladness,
Saw and pitied that mournful boy,   50
And I swore to take his gloomy sadness
And give to him my beamy joy –

'Heavy and dark the night is closing,
Heavy and dark may its biding be,
Better for all from grief reposing,   55
And better for all who watch like me –

'Guardian angel, he lacks no longer;
Evil fortune he need not fear;
Fate is strong but love is stronger
And more unsleeping than angel's care –'   60

The Prisoner

A Fragment

In the dungeon-crypts, idly did I stray,
Reckless of the lives wasting there away;
'Draw the ponderous bars! open, Warder stern!'
He dared not say me nay – the hinges harshly turn.

'Our guests are darkly lodged,' I whisper'd, gazing through   5
The vault, whose grated eye showed heaven more grey than
    blue;
(This was when glad spring laughed in awaking pride;)
'Aye, darkly lodged enough!' returned my sullen guide.

Then, God forgive my youth; forgive my careless tongue;
I scoffed, as the chill chains on the damp flag-stones rung: 10
'Confined in triple walls, art thou so much to fear,
That we must bind thee down and clench thy fetters here?'

The captive raised her face, it was as soft and mild
As sculptured marble saint, or slumbering unwean'd child;
It was so soft and mild, it was so sweet and fair,   15
Pain could not trace a line, nor grief a shadow there!

The captive raised her hand and pressed it to her brow;
'I have been struck,' she said, 'and I am suffering now;
Yet these are little worth, your bolts and irons strong,
And, were they forged in steel, they could not hold me long.'   20

Hoarse laughed the jailor grim: 'Shall I be won to hear;
Dost think, fond, dreaming wretch, that I shall grant thy prayer?
Or, better still, wilt melt my master's heart with groans?
Ah! sooner might the sun thaw down these granite stones.

'My master's voice is low, his aspect bland and kind,   25
But hard as hardest flint, the soul that lurks behind;
And I am rough and rude, yet not more rough to see
Than is the hidden ghost that has its home in me.'

About her lips there played a smile of almost scorn,
'My friend,' she gently said, 'you have not heard me mourn;   30
When you my kindred's lives, *my* lost life, can restore,
Then may I weep and sue, – but never, friend, before!

Still, let my tyrants know, I am not doomed to wear
Year after year in gloom, and desolate despair;
A messenger of Hope, comes every night to me,   35
And offers for short life, eternal liberty.

He comes with western winds, with evening's wandering airs,
With that clear dusk of heaven that brings the thickest stars.
Winds take a pensive tone, and stars a tender fire,
And visions rise, and change, that kill me with desire.   40

Desire for nothing known in my maturer years,
When Joy grew mad with awe, at counting future tears.
When, if my spirit's sky was full of flashes warm,
I knew not whence they came, from sun, or thunder storm.

But, first, a hush of peace – a soundless calm descends;   45
The struggle of distress, and fierce impatience ends.
Mute music soothes my breast, unuttered harmony,
That I could never dream, till Earth was lost to me.

Then dawns the Invisible; the Unseen its truth reveals;
My outward sense is gone, my inward essence feels: 50
Its wings are almost free – its home, its harbour found,
Measuring the gulph, it stoops, and dares the final bound.

Oh, dreadful is the check – intense the agony –
When the ear begins to hear, and the eye begins to see;
When the pulse begins to throb, the brain to think again,   55
The soul to feel the flesh, and the flesh to feel the chain.

Yet I would lose no sting, would wish no torture less,
The more that anguish racks, the earlier it will bless;
And robed in fires of hell, or bright with heavenly shine,
If it but herald death, the vision is divine!'   60

She ceased to speak, and we, unanswering, turned to go –
We had no further power to work the captive woe:
Her cheek, her gleaming eye, declared that man had given
A sentence, unapproved, and overruled by Heaven.

'No coward soul is mine'

No coward soul is mine,
No trembler in the world's storm-troubled sphere,
I see Heaven's glories shine
And Faith shines equal arming me from Fear.

O God within my breast,   5
Almighty ever-present Deity,
Life, that in me hast rest
As I Undying Life, have power in thee.

Vain are the thousand creeds
That move men's hearts, unutterably vain,   10
Worthless as withered weeds
Or idlest froth amid the boundless main

To waken doubt in one
Holding so fast by thy infinity,
So surely anchored on   15
The steadfast rock of Immortality.

With wide-embracing love
Thy spirit animates eternal years,
Pervades and broods above,
Changes, sustains, dissolves, creates and rears.   20

Though Earth and moon were gone
And suns and universes ceased to be
And thou wert left alone,
Every Existence would exist in thee.

There is not room for Death   25
Nor atom that his might could render void
Since thou art Being and Breath
And what thou art may never be destroyed.

Anne Brontë

The Bluebell

A fine and subtle spirit dwells
   In every little flower,
Each one its own sweet feeling breathes
   With more or less of power.

There is a silent eloquence   5
   In every wild bluebell,
That fills my softened heart with bliss
   That words could never tell.

Yet I recall, not long ago,
   A bright and sunny day: 10
'Twas when I led a toilsome life
   So many leagues away.

That day along a sunny road
   All carelessly I strayed
Between two banks where smiling flowers   15
   Their varied hues displayed.

Before me rose a lofty hill,
   Behind me lay the sea;
My heart was not so heavy then
   As it was wont to be.   20

Less harassed than at other times
   I saw the scene was fair,
And spoke and laughed to those around,
   As if I knew no care.

But as I looked upon the bank,   25
   My wandering glances fell

Upon a little trembling flower,
   A single sweet bluebell.

Whence came that rising in my throat,
   That dimness in my eyes?   30
Why did those burning drops distil,
   Those bitter feelings rise?

Oh, that lone flower recalled to me
   My happy childhood's hours,
When bluebells seemed like fairy gifts,   35
   A prize among the flowers.

Those sunny days of merriment
   When heart and soul were free,
And when I dwelt with kindred hearts
   That loved and cared for me.   40

I had not then mid heartless crowds
   To spend a thankless life,
In seeking after others' weal
   With anxious toil and strife.

'Sad wanderer, weep those blissful times   45
   That never may return!'
The lovely floweret seemed to say,
   And thus it made me mourn.

Appeal

Oh, I am very weary,
   Though tears no longer flow;
My eyes are tired of weeping,
   My heart is sick of woe;

My life is very lonely,   5
   My days pass heavily,
I'm weary of repining,
   Wilt thou not come to me?

Oh, didst thou know my longings
   For thee, from day to day,   10
My hopes, so often blighted,
   Thou wouldst not thus delay!

Lines Written at Thorp Green

That summer sun, whose genial glow
Now cheers my drooping spirit so,
   Must cold and silent be,
And only light our northern clime
With feeble ray, before the time   5
   I long so much to see.

And this soft, whispering breeze, that now
So gently cools my fevered brow,
   This too, alas! must turn
To a wild blast, whose icy dart   10
Pierces and chills me to the heart,
   Before I cease to mourn.

And these bright flowers I love so well,
Verbena, rose, and sweet bluebell,
   Must droop and die away;   15
Those thick, green leaves, with all their shade
And rustling music, they must fade,
   And every one decay.

But if the sunny, summer time,
And woods and meadows in their prime,   20
   Are sweet to them that roam:
Far sweeter is the winter bare,

With long, dark nights, and landscape drear,
  To them that are at Home!

Despondency

I have gone backward in the work,
  The labour has not sped;
Drowsy and dark my spirit lies,
  Heavy and dull as lead.

How can I rouse my sinking soul   5
  From such a lethargy?
How can I break these iron chains
  And set my spirit free?

There have been times when I have mourned
  In anguish o'er the past,   10
And raised my suppliant hands on high,
  While tears fell thick and fast;

And prayed to have my sins forgiven,
  With such a fervent zeal,
An earnest grief and strong desire,   15
  As now I cannot feel!

And vowed to trample on my sins,
  And called on Heaven to aid
My spirit in her firm resolves
  And hear the vows I made.   20

And I have felt so full of love,
  So strong in spirit then,
As if my heart would never cool,
  Or wander back again.

And yet, alas! how many times   25
   My feet have gone astray!
How oft have I forgot my God,
   How greatly fallen away!

My sins increase, my love grows cold,
   And Hope within me dies: 30
And Faith itself is wavering now;
   Oh, how shall I arise!

I cannot weep but I can pray,
   Then let me not despair;
Lord Jesus, save me lest I die   35
   And hear a wretch's prayer.

In Memory of a Happy Day
in February

Blessed be Thou for all the joy
   My soul has felt today!
Oh, let its memory stay with me
   And never pass away!

I was alone, for those I loved   5
   Were far away from me;
The sun shone on the withered grass,
   The wind blew fresh and free.

Was it the smile of early spring
   That made my bosom glow?   10
'Twas sweet, but neither sun nor wind
   Could raise my spirit so.

Was it some feeling of delight,
   All vague and undefined?

No, 'twas a rapture deep and strong,   15
   Expanding in my mind!

Was it a sanguine view of life
   And all its transient bliss –
A hope of bright prosperity?
   Oh, no, it was not this!   20

It was a glimpse of truths divine
   Unto my spirit given,
Illumined by a ray of light
   That shone direct from Heaven!

I knew there was a God on high   25
   By whom all things were made;
I saw His wisdom and His power
   In all His works displayed.

But most throughout the moral world
   I saw His glory shine;   30
I saw His wisdom infinite,
   His mercy all divine.

Deep secrets of His providence
   In darkness long concealed,
Were brought to my delighted eyes   35
   And graciously revealed.

And while I wondered and adored
   His wisdom so divine,
I did not tremble at His power:
   I felt that God was mine.   40

I knew that my Redeemer lived;
   I did not fear to die;
I felt that I should rise again
   To immortality.

I longed to view that bliss divine   45
   Which eye hath never seen;
To see the glories of His face
   Without the veil between.

Lines Composed in a Wood on a Windy Day

My soul is awakened, my spirit is soaring
And carried aloft on the wings of the breeze;
For above and around me the wild wind is roaring,
Arousing to rapture the earth and the seas.

The long withered grass in the sunshine is glancing,   5
The bare trees are tossing their branches on high;
The dead leaves, beneath them, are merrily dancing,
The white clouds are scudding across the blue sky.

I wish I could see how the ocean is lashing
The foam of its billows to whirlwinds of spray;   10
I wish I could see how its proud waves are dashing,
And hear the wild roar of their thunder today!

The Captive Dove

Poor restless dove, I pity thee;
And when I hear thy plaintive moan,
I mourn for thy captivity,
And in thy woes forget mine own.

To see thee stand prepared to fly,   5
And flap those useless wings of thine,
And gaze into the distant sky,
Would melt a harder heart than mine.

In vain – in vain! Thou canst not rise:
Thy prison roof confines thee there;   10
Its slender wires delude thine eyes,
And quench thy longings with despair.

Oh, thou wert made to wander free
In sunny mead and shady grove,
And, far beyond the rolling sea,   15
In distant climes, at will to rove!

Yet, hadst thou but one gentle mate
Thy little drooping heart to cheer,
And share with thee thy captive state,
Thou couldst be happy even there.   20

Yes, even there, if, listening by,
One faithful dear companion stood,
While gazing on her full bright eye,
Thou mightst forget thy native wood.

But thou, poor solitary dove,   25
Must make, unheard, thy joyless moan;
The heart, that Nature formed to love,
Must pine, neglected, and alone.

The Consolation

Though bleak these woods, and damp the ground
With fallen leaves so thickly strown,
And cold the wind that wanders round
With wild and melancholy moan;

There *is* a friendly roof, I know,   5
Might shield me from the wintry blast;
There is a fire, whose ruddy glow
Will cheer me for my wanderings past.

And so, though still, where'er I go,
Cold stranger-glances meet my eye;   10
Though, when my spirit sinks in woe,
Unheeded swells the unbidden sigh:

Though solitude, endured too long,
Bids youthful joys too soon decay,
Makes mirth a stranger to my tongue,   15
And overclouds my noon of day;

When kindly thoughts, that would have way,
Flow back discouraged to my breast; –
I know there *is*, though far away,
A home where heart and soul may rest.   20

Warm hands are there, that, clasped in mine,
The warmer heart will not belie;
While mirth, and truth, and friendship shine
In smiling lip and earnest eye.

The ice that gathers round my heart   25
May there be thawed; and sweetly, then,
The joys of youth, that now depart,
Will come to cheer my soul again.

Though far I roam, that thought shall be
My hope, my comfort, everywhere;   30
While such a home remains to me,
My heart shall never know despair!

A Reminiscence

Yes, thou art gone! and never more
Thy sunny smile shall gladden me;
But I may pass the old church door,
And pace the floor that covers thee,

May stand upon the cold, damp stone,   5
And think that, frozen, lies below
The lightest heart that I have known,
The kindest I shall ever know.

Yet, though I cannot see thee more,
'Tis still a comfort to have seen;   10
And though thy transient life is o'er,
'Tis sweet to think that thou hast been;

To think a soul so near divine,
Within a form, so angel fair,
United to a heart like thine,   15
Has gladdened once our humble sphere.

Memory

Brightly the sun of summer shone,
Green fields and waving woods upon,
    And soft winds wandered by;
Above, a sky of purest blue,
Around, bright flowers of loveliest hue,   5
    Allured the gazer's eye.

But what were all these charms to me,
When one sweet breath of memory
    Came gently wafting by?
I closed my eyes against the day,   10
And called my willing soul away,
    From earth, and air, and sky;

That I might simply fancy there
One little flower – a primrose fair,
    Just opening into sight;   15
As in the days of infancy,
An opening primrose seemed to me
    A source of strange delight.

Sweet Memory! ever smile on me;
Nature's chief beauties spring from thee;   20

Oh, still thy tribute bring!
Still make the golden crocus shine
Among the flowers the most divine.
    The glory of the spring.

Still in the wall-flower's fragrance dwell;   25
And hover round the slight blue bell,
    My childhood's darling flower.
Smile on the little daisy still,
The buttercup's bright goblet fill
    With all thy former power.   30

For ever hang thy dreamy spell
Round mountain star and heather bell,
    And do not pass away
From sparkling frost, of wreathed snow,
And whisper when the wild winds blow,   35
    Or rippling waters play.

Is childhood, then, so all divine?
Or Memory, is the glory thine,
    That haloes thus the past?
Not *all* divine; its pangs of grief,   40
(Although, perchance, their stay be brief,)
    Are bitter while they last.

Nor is the glory all thine own,
For on our earliest joys alone
    That holy light is cast.   45
With such a ray, no spell of thine
Can make our later pleasures shine,
    Though long ago they passed.

A Prayer

My God! Oh let me call Thee mine!
　　Weak, wretched sinner though I be,
My trembling soul would fain be Thine,
　　My feeble faith still clings to Thee.

Not only for the past I grieve,   5
　　The future fills me with dismay;
Unless Thou hasten to relieve,
　　I know my heart will fall away.

I cannot say my faith is strong,
　　I dare not hope my love is great,   10
But strength and love to Thee belong,
　　Oh do not leave me desolate!

I know I owe my all to Thee.
　　Oh! take the heart I cannot give.
Do Thou my Strength, my Saviour be: 15
　　And make me to Thy glory live!

Home

How brightly glistening in the sun
　　The woodland ivy plays!
While yonder beeches from their barks
　　Reflect his silver rays.

That sun surveys a lovely scene   5
　　From softly smiling skies:
And wildly through unnumbered trees
　　The wind of winter sighs:

Now loud, it thunders o'er my head,
　　And now in distance dies.   10

But give me back my barren hills
　　Where colder breezes rise;

Where scarce the scattered, stunted trees
　　Can yield an answering swell,
But where a wilderness of heath   15
　　Returns the sound as well.

For yonder garden, fair and wide,
　　With groves of evergreen,
Long winding walks, and borders trim,
　　And velvet lawns between;   20

Restore to me that little spot,
　　With grey walls compassed round,
Where knotted grass neglected lies,
　　And weeds usurp the ground.

Though all around this mansion high   25
　　Invites the foot to roam,
And though its halls are fair within –
　　Oh, give me back my HOME!

Dreams

While on my lonely couch I lie,
　　I seldom feel my self alone,
For fancy fills my dreaming eye
　　With scenes and pleasures of its own.

Then I may cherish at my breast   5
　　An infant's form beloved and fair;
May smile and soothe it into rest,
　　With all a mother's fondest care.

How sweet to feel its helpless form
   Depending thus on me alone;   10
And while I hold it safe and warm,
   What bliss to think it is my own!

And glances then may meet my eyes
   That daylight never showed to me;
What raptures in my bosom rise   15
   Those earnest looks of love to see!

To feel my hand so kindly pressed,
   To know myself beloved at last;
To think my heart has found a rest,
   My life of solitude is past!   20

But then to wake and find it flown,
   The dream of happiness destroyed;
To find myself unloved, alone,
   What tongue can speak the dreary void!

A heart whence warm affections flow,   25
   Creator, Thou hast given to me;
And am I only thus to know
   How sweet the joys of love would be?

If This Be All

O God! if this indeed be all
   That Life can show to me;
If on my aching brow may fall
   No freshening dew from Thee, –

If with no brighter light than this   5
   The lamp of hope may glow,
And I may only *dream* of bliss,
   And wake to weary woe;

If friendship's solace must decay,
    When other joys are gone,   10
And love must keep so far away,
    While I go wandering on, –

Wandering and toiling without gain,
    The slave of others' will,
With constant care, and frequent pain,   15
    Despised, forgotten still;

Grieving to look on vice and sin,
    Yet powerless to quell
The silent current from within,
    The outward torrent's swell: 20

While all the good I would impart,
    The feelings I would share,
Are driven backward to my heart,
    And turned to wormwood, there;

If clouds must *ever* keep from sight   25
    The glories of the Sun,
And I must suffer Winter's blight,
    Ere Summer is begun;

If Life must be so full of care,
    Then call me soon to Thee;   30
Or give me strength enough to bear
    My load of misery.

The Penitent

I mourn with thee, and yet rejoice
    That thou shouldst sorrow so;
With angel choirs I join my voice
    To bless the sinner's woe.

Though friends and kindred turn away,   5
    And laugh thy grief to scorn;
I hear the great Redeemer say,
    'Blessed are ye that mourn.'

Hold on thy course, nor deem it strange
    That earthly cords are riven: 10
Man may lament the wondrous change,
    But 'there is joy in heaven!'

'Oh, they have robbed me of the hope'

Oh, they have robbed me of the hope
    My spirit held so dear;
They will not let me hear that voice
    My soul delights to hear.

They will not let me see that face   5
    I so delight to see;
And they have taken all thy smiles,
    And all thy love from me.

Well, let them seize on all they can; –
    One treasure still is mine, –   10
A heart that loves to think on thee,
    And feels the worth of thine.

The Arbour

I'll rest me in this sheltered bower,
And look upon the clear blue sky
That smiles upon me through the trees,
Which stand so thickly clustering by;

And view their green and glossy leaves,   5
All glistening in the sunshine fair;
And list the rustling of their boughs,
So softly whispering through the air.

And while my ear drinks in the sound,
My winged soul shall fly away;   10
Reviewing long departed years
As one mild, beaming, autumn day;

And soaring on to future scenes,
Like hills and woods, and valleys green,
All basking in the summer's sun,   15
But distant still, and dimly seen.

Oh, list! 'tis summer's very breath
That gently shakes the rustling trees –
But look! the snow is on the ground –
How can I think of scenes like these?   20

'Tis but the *frost* that clears the air,
And gives the sky that lovely blue;
They're smiling in a *winter's* sun,
Those evergreens of sombre hue.

And winter's chill is on my heart –   25
How can I dream of future bliss?
How can my spirit soar away,
Confined by such a chain as this?

Last Lines

A dreadful darkness closes in
   On my bewildered mind;
O let me suffer and not sin,
   Be tortured yet resigned.

Through all this world of blinding mist 5
   Still let me look to thee,
And give me courage to resist
   The Tempter till he flee.

Weary I am – O give me strength,
   And leave me not to faint, 10
Say thou wilt comfort me at length
   And pity my complaint.

I've begged to serve thee heart and soul,
   To sacrifice to thee
No niggard portion, but the whole 15
   Of my identity.

I hoped amid the brave and strong
   My portioned task might lie,
To toil amid the labouring throng
   With purpose keen and high; 20

But thou hast fixed another part,
   And thou hast fixed it well.
I said so with my breaking heart
   When first the anguish fell.

O thou hast taken my delight 25
   And hope of life away,
And bid me watch the painful night
   And wait the weary day.

The hope and the delight were thine,
   I bless thee for their loan; 30

I gave thee while I deemed them mine
    Too little thanks, I own.

Shall I with joy thy blessings share
    And not endure their loss,
Or hope the martyr's crown to wear   35
    And cast away the cross?

These weary hours will not be lost,
    These days of passive misery,
These nights of darkness anguish-tost,
    If I can fix my heart on thee.   40

The wretch that weak and weary lies
    Crushed with sorrow, worn with pain,
Still to Heaven may lift his eyes
    And strive and labour not in vain.

Weak and weary though I lie   45
    Crushed with sorrow, worn with pain,
I may lift to Heaven mine eye
    And strive and labour not in vain.

That inward strife against the sins
    That ever wait on suffering   50
To watch and strike where first begins
    Each ill that would corruption bring;

That secret labour to sustain
    With humble patience every blow,
To gather fortitude from pain   55
    And hope and holiness from woe.

Thus let me serve thee from my heart
    Whatever be my written fate,
Whether thus early to depart
    Or yet awhile to wait.   60

If thou shouldst bring me back to life,
    More humbled I should be,

More wise, more strengthened for the strife,
    More apt to lean on thee.

Should Death be standing at the gate   65
    Thus should I keep my vow,
But hard whate'er my future fate,
    So let me serve thee now.

Notes

Abbreviated references in notes:

AB: *The Complete Poems of Anne Brontë*, ed. Clement Shorter (London, 1920).

BPM: Brontë Parsonage Museum, Bonnell Manuscripts.

CB: *The Poems of Charlotte Brontë*, ed. Tom Winnifrith (Shakespeare Head Press, Oxford, 1984).

EJB: facsimile of Emily Jane Brontë (Honresfeld) MS in *The Poems of Emily Jane Brontë and Anne Brontë* (Shakespeare Head Press, Oxford, 1934).

EJB/A: Emily Jane Brontë, MS Ashley 175, British Library.

EJB/G: Emily Jane Brontë, Gondal MS Add. 43483, British Library.

PBB: *The Poems of Patrick Branwell Brontë*, ed. Tom Winnifrith (Shakespeare Head Press, Oxford, 1983).

PBB/H: *The Odes of Quintus Horatius Flaccus, Book 1*, trans. Patrick Branwell Brontë, intro. John Drinkwater (London, 1923).

1846: *Poems* by Currer, Ellis, and Acton Bell (London, 1846).

Texts: spelling in manuscript texts has been silently corrected, and punctuation inserted and/or modernised. Arranged chronologically for each author.

Charlotte Brontë

from **Retrospection** (19 December 1835), an extract from a longer poem which concludes with a prose section. Written while CB was teaching at Roe Head, it celebrates the fictitious worlds that she and her three siblings had invented since early childhood, particularly the kingdom of Angria which CB shared with Branwell. Text: **CB**.

The Teacher's Monologue (15 May 1837), written at Roe Head soon after

CB had received the poet Southey's letter telling her that 'Literature cannot be the business of a woman's life . . .'. Text: **1846.**

Mementos (early drafts, probably June–July 1837). An old servant recounts a gothic tale of masculine delinquence and female suffering, typical of CB's fictions at this period. Text: **1846**.

Parting (29 January 1838). Written on the last day of the Christmas holidays before CB returned to teaching. Text: **1846**.

Life (26 March 1839). Text: **1846**.

'The Autumn day its course has run' (undated, probably spring 1845). A fragment from CB's Brussels exercise book which persuasively recreates the pensive tranquillity of an autumn evening. Text: **BPM** 118.

'Early wrapt in slumber deep' (undated, probably spring 1845). Unusually laconic for CB, the poem is nevertheless richly suggestive, linking sleep with the passing of time, deftly sketching the social hierarchy at the dreaming house, and evoking its beautiful natural setting. Text: **CB**.

'He saw my heart's woe' (undated, but appears on back of letter dated 13 November 1847). Almost certainly draws on CB's passionate responses to her mentor and colleague, Constantin Heger, when she was studying and teaching in Brussels. Text: **CB**.

On the Death of Emily Jane Brontë (24 December 1848). Emily died on 19 December 1848 after resolutely refusing medical care or any change in her routines to accommodate her increasing weakness. Text: **CB**.

On the Death of Anne Brontë (21 June 1849). Anne died on 28 May 1849, in Scarborough, where she had gone for the bracing air and a last look at the sea she loved. Text: **CB**.

Patrick Branwell Brontë

Augusta (spring 1834). Augusta di Segovia was the first wife of one of PBB's favourite Angrian heroes, Alexander Percy, Earl of Northangerland. Text: **PBB**.

Lines (1834). Ostensibly written by the young Percy, to set to music. Text: **PBB**.

Memory (undated; possibly July / August 1836). Opposite an earlier draft, Branwell had written: 'I am more terrifically and infernally and Idiotically and Brutally STUPID – than ever I was in the whole course of my incarnate existence The above precious lines are the fruits of one hours most agonising labour between ½ past 6 and ½ past 7 on the evening of Wednesday, July 1836.' Text: **PBB**.

'Oh, all our cares' (undated; possibly summer 1836). Text: **PBB**.

'The man who will not know another' (undated; possibly 1836/7). In his memoir of PBB in *Pictures of the Past* (London. 1879), Francis Grundy claims this poem as a spontaneous effusion 'because [Branwell] thought I was disposed to treat him distantly at a party' (p. 78). The existence of earlier drafts contradicts Grundy's theory that this was an impromptu piece, but demonstrates PBB's readiness to fit his poetry to a suitable occasion. Text: **PBB**.

On Caroline (undated; possibly 1837). May refer to PBB's memories of his dead sister Maria. Text: **PBB**.

'Now – but one moment, let me stay' (undated; possibly 1837). Text: **PBB**.

Death Triumphant (May, 1838). Text: **PBB**.

To Sestius Ode IV of PBB's translations of the Odes of Horace. which PBB probably began in spring 1838 and polished January to June, 1840. Text: **PBB/H**.

'Oh Thou, whose beams were most withdrawn' (8 August 1841). Text: **PBB**.

'O God! while I in pleasure's wiles' (19 December 1841). Text: **PBB**.

Peaceful Death and Painful Life (undated). Written in PBB's Northangerland persona, and published by the *Halifax Guardian* on 14 May 1842. May have been revised from an earlier version. Text: **PBB**.

Thorp Green (30 March 1843). Written soon after PBB went to Thorp Green as tutor to Edmund Robinson. Text: **PBB**.

Penmænmawr (Probably July–November 1845). PBB visited North Wales in late July and sent the poem to his friend J. B. Leyland in a letter dated 25 November 1845. Text: **PBB**.

Epistle From a Father to a Child in Her Grave (3 April 1846). In her biography, *The Brontës* (London, 1994), Juliet Barker discusses the rumour that PBB 'left Mr Postlethwaites with a natural child . . . which died', and suggests that this poem may well be autobiographical (see Barker. pp. 333–5). Text: **PBB**.

Emily Jane Brontë

'Will the day be bright or cloudy?' (12 July 1836). The destiny of a newborn girl can be foretold from the weather on the day of her birth. Text: **BPM** 127.

'Tell me, tell me, smiling child' (undated). Here, a child describes her own past. present and future in terms of the natural world. Text: **BPM** 127.

'Alone I sat' (August 1837). Text: **BPM** 127.

Lines ('Far away is the land of rest') (October 1837). Text: **EJB/A**.

Lines ('I die, but when the grave shall press') (December, 1837). Text: **EJB/A**.

To a Wreath of Snow by A. G. Almeda (December, 1837). Augusta Almeda, Queen of Gondal, reveals her independent spirit even when in prison. The 'wreath' is presumably a fall of snow that has banked up against her high dungeon window. and gleams through the drab morning light. Text: **EJB/A**.

Song to A. A. (May. 1838). Elderno lake is one of the Gondal locations; A. A. is otherwise unidentified. Text: **EJB/A**.

Song by Julius Brenzaida to G. S. (17 October 1838). Julius Brenzaida becomes Emperor of Gondal and its satellite island Gaaldine; Geraldine is one of his two lovers. Text: **EJB/G**.

F. De Samara to A. G. A. (1 November 1838). Fernando de Samara's last words to Augusta before he commits suicide for her sake. Text: **EJB/G**.

'Loud without the wind was roaring' (11 November 1838). Written while EJB was teaching at Law Hill. it may have a personal or a Gondal reference. Text: **EJB**.

'The blue bell is the sweetest flower' (18 December 1838). Text: **EJB**.

Song ('King Julius left the south country') (20 April 1839). Threatens the downfall of Julius Brenzaida. Text: **EJB/A**.

'Come hither, child' (19 July 1839). Ula is a province of Gaaldine. Text: **BPM** 127.

Song (**'O between distress and pleasure'**) (15 October 1839). Text: **EJB/A**.

'Love is like the wild rose briar' (undated; possibly October / November 1839). Text: **EJB**.

'Come, walk with me' (undated). Text: **EJB/G**.

Stanzas (4 May 1840). Text: **1846**.

'If grief for grief can touch thee' (18 May 1840). Text: **EJB**.

The Night-Wind (11 September 1840). Text: **EJB**.

The Old Stoic (1 March 1841). One of EJB's most famous poems, it was recorded in the Honresfeld notebook, which suggests it may have a personal rather than a Gondal reference. Text: **1846**.

To A. G. A. (undated; maybe summer 1843). Addressed to the Queen of Gondal, Augusta Almeda, who characteristically defends her right not to stay faithful to only one lover. Text: **EJB/G**.

Hope (18 December 1843). Text: **1846**.

Song (**'The linnet in the rocky dells'**) (1 May 1844). Written in the persona of Lord Eldred W., Augusta's friend and faithful servant. In her reconstruction of EJB's Gondal narratives, *Gondal's Queen*, Fannie Ratchford describes this poem as expressing Lord Eldred's long mourning after he finds the murdered queen's body. Text: **1846**.

To Imagination (3 September 1844). Text: **1846**.

A Death-Scene (2 December 1844). A Gondal poem, from Augusta to her first husband, Lord of Elbë. The Gondal references were deleted or obscured for the 1846 edition of the *Poems*. Text: **1846**.

Remembrance (3 March 1845). The lament of Rosina Alcona for her lover, Julius Brenzaida, this is one of the great English love poems, remarkable alike for its strong sense of loss, for the stoicism of the survivor, and EJB's metrical fluency. Text: **1846**.

Death (10 April 1845). Text: **1846**.

Stars (14 April 1845). Text: **1846**.

A. E. and R. C. (28 May 1845). A Gondal poem; A. E. may refer to Alexander of Elbë. Text: **EJB/G**.

The Prisoner (9 October 1845). An account of the loss of self associated with mysticism, apparently framed by a Gondal narrative. Text: **1846**.

'No coward soul is mine' (2 January 1846). Whatever the autobiographical content of this poem, and it does appear in EJB's personal rather than her Gondal notebook, it is an extraordinarily self-confident assertion of personal belief by a young woman, daughter of a clergyman, living more or less in intellectual isolation in the mid-nineteenth century. Text: **EJB**.

Anne Brontë

The Bluebell (22 August 1840). Written a few months after Anne had gone as governess to the Robinson family at Thorp Green, the poem perhaps expresses her depression and feelings of confinement away from home. Text: **AB**.

Appeal (28 August 1840). The manuscript title was 'Lines written at Thorp Green'. Whether Anne was thinking of her family, particularly Emily, or writing as a Gondal character, can only be conjectured. Text: **1846**.

Lines Written at Thorp Green (19 August 1841). Demonstrates Anne's characteristic love of flowers and profound homesickness. Text: **AB**.

Despondency (20 December 1841). Several of AB's poems record the struggle for faith in terms reminiscent of Christina Rossetti (writing several decades later). Text: **AB** and **BPM** 134.

In Memory of a Happy Day in February (begun February, finished 10 November 1842). AB's confident assertion of faith in life after death. Text: **AB** and **BPM** 134.

Lines Composed in a Wood on a Windy Day (30 December 1842). AB wrote on the manuscript: 'Composed in the Long-Plantation on a wild bright windy day.' Text: **1846**.

The Captive Dove (31 October 1843, but AB notes: 'Mostly written in the spring of 1842.'). AB's ready sympathy for a fellow-creature imprisoned like herself: she was still working at Thorp Green. Text: **1846**.

The Consolation (7 November 1843). Text: **1846**.

A Reminiscence (April 1844). It may be that Anne was thinking of her father's merry-hearted curate, William Weightman, who had died of cholera in September 1842, but there is no evidence to suggest an attachment apart from some tart references by Charlotte, and Anne had other dead, real and imaginary, to mourn. Text: **1846**.

Memory (29 May 1844). Text: **1846**.

A Prayer (13 October 1844). Again, a pale reflection of Christina Rossetti's passionate 'Nay pierce, nay probe, nay dig within, / Probe my quick core and sound my depth' ('The heart knoweth its own bitterness'), and John Donne's equally explicit 'Batter my heart, three-personed God': 'for I / Except you enthral me, never shall be free, / Nor ever chaste, except you ravish me.' Self-controlled even in her private writings, AB's expression was less forceful, but probably her longing to be claimed by God was none the less heartfelt. Text: **BPM 134**.

Home (undated). Text: **1846**.

Dreams (spring 1845). Text: **AB**.

If This Be All (20 May 1845). Text: **1846**.

The Penitent (1845). Text: **1846**.

'Oh, they have robbed me of the hope' (undated). Published in Anne's first novel, *Agnes Grey* (1847). Text: **AB**.

The Arbour (undated). Text: **1846**.

Last Lines (7 and 28 January 1849). Written soon after EJB's death, and when Anne had just been diagnosed as also suffering from tubercular consumption. Text: **BPM 137**.

Acknowledgements

I would like to thank the following for permission to use texts: Blackwell Publishers for poems from Tom Winnifrith's editions of *The Poems of Charlotte Brontë* and *The Poems of Patrick Branwell Brontë*. I would also like to thank the British Library and the Brontë Society for permission to use manuscript texts. Thanks are also due to Kathryn White at the Brontë Parsonage Museum for her customary helpfulness, and to Hilary Laurie and her editors at Everyman, who are always such a pleasure to work with.